Money Markets

MONEY MARKETS

Brian Coyle

FINANCIAL WORLD Publishing
THE CHARTERED INSTITUTE OF BANKERS

Financial World Publishing
IFS House
4-9 Burgate Lane
Canterbury
Kent
CT1 2XJ
United Kingdom

Telephone: 01227 818687

Financial World Publishing publications are published by
The Chartered Institute of Bankers, a non-profit making registered educational charity.

Typeset by Kevin O'Connor
Printed in Italy

ISBN 0-85297-441-8

Contents

1

Introduction

The money markets are financial markets for transactions in wholesale short-term loans and deposits, and for trading short-term financial instruments. Short term means having a maturity or term of up to 12 months or so, although many money-market transactions are overnight, from one day to the next, and most transactions have a maturity of three months or less. Money markets exist to meet the needs of financial institutions and companies seeking short-term funding or with a short-term surplus of funds to lend or invest for a limited period.

Money markets can be distinguished from capital markets and derivatives markets.

- Capital markets are the markets for long-term finance, and include markets for equities and bonds. Capital markets and money markets are both cash markets, because transactions consist of the delivery of an item by a borrower to a lender or investor who settles the transaction with a payment in cash.
- Derivatives markets are markets for financial instruments that are derived from a transaction in an underlying money market or capital-market instrument. Derivative instruments include forward-rate agreements (FRAs), futures, options and swaps.

The Constituent Money Markets

The principal money markets in large financial centers such as New York and London are:

- the interbank market, for short-term loans and deposits

- the eurocurrency market
- the markets in discount instruments that are principally Treasury bills, bank bills and trade bills
- the market in Certificates of Deposit
- the commercial paper (CP) market
- the market for sale and repurchase agreements (the repo market).

These are all over-the-counter markets, in the sense that trading or dealing is not conducted in a single location on an exchange floor. Rather, the markets consist of a huge web of interconnected direct dealing lines, telephone lines and computer links at offices of banks, brokers, other financial institutions and large and medium-sized non-bank companies.

Foreign-exchange markets (FX markets) also might be described as money markets. FX markets are for buying and selling currencies but there are close links between FX markets and eurocurrency markets, where currencies are borrowed and lent short-term. Exchange rates for forward exchange contracts depend on the interest-rate differentials between currencies in the eurocurrency market.

Who Uses Money Markets?

Money markets are used by organizations that need to borrow short-term, and organizations with funds to lend or invest short-term. These are mainly banks and investment institutions but also include government agencies, and industrial and commercial companies. Participants in the market fall into three broad categories:

- borrowers
- lenders/investors, and
- intermediaries such as money brokers, bringing borrowers and lenders/investors together. Some financial institutions specialize in money-market transactions, buying and selling money-market instruments, or accepting short-term cash deposits and re-investing the funds in short-term instruments.

Banks may operate on one side of the market at a particular time, borrowing the amount they require or lending their available surplus to one or more other participants in the market. Alternatively, banks might buy money-market instruments such as bills or CDs to invest surplus funds, or sell their holdings of these instruments to raise funds.

Money markets are important for the commercial banking system. Banks settle a large proportion of the payment transactions of their customers by transferring funds between their accounts at a central bank. In addition, payments between bank customers and the government, for example payments of tax, are settled by the banks with the government through their account at the central bank. At any time, individual banks might have a shortage or a surplus of funds. Interbank transactions, to borrow short-term to fund a shortage and lend short-term to earn interest income from a surplus, are an important feature of money-market operations.

Money markets also are significant because interest rates in these markets affect interest rates in other banking operations, particularly bank lending. The central government of many countries, including those of the US, European Union euro zone and the UK, conduct money-market operations in the markets as a means of influencing the level of interest rates in their domestic economy.

Summary

Overview of the Money Markets

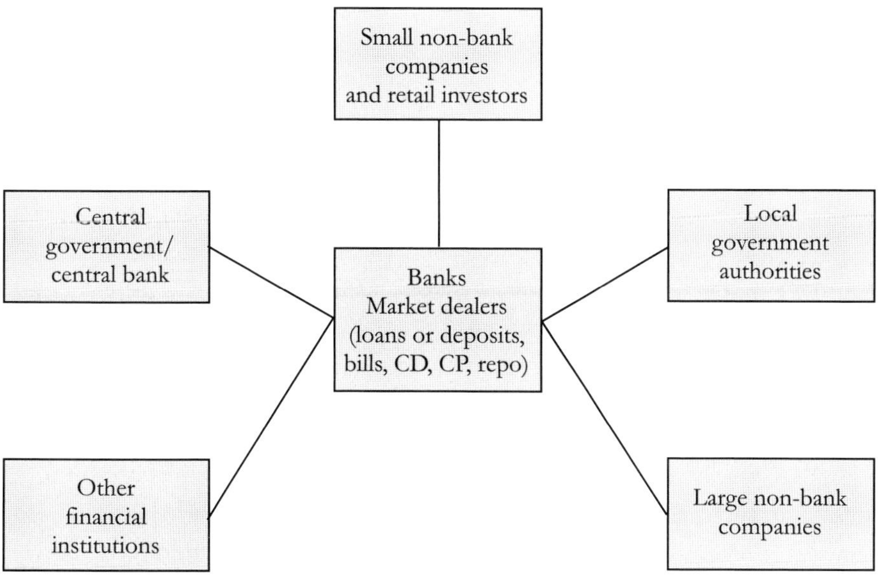

The Interbank Market

Role of the Interbank Market

An interbank market is a market for wholesale loans and deposits, primarily between banks. Wholesale does not have an exact definition, but typical transactions are unlikely to be less than about $15 million.

Interbank borrowing and lending is short term. Short-term means for up to about 12 months, but the bulk of activity is confined to three months or less. Despite its name, participation in the interbank market need not be confined to banks, although most activity will come from commercial banks. Other financial institutions such as insurance companies and pension funds and discount houses might be active in the market, as well as larger companies that deal direct with other money-market participants.

The need for interbank lending arises because some commercial banks will have a surplus of funds on a particular day, and other banks will have a deficit. Cash withdrawn or transferred from one customer account usually will end up in the account of another customer, often at a different bank. Even if the total amount of money in the commercial banking system were to remain constant, there would be movements of money between the banks. Surplus funds are invested or lent, and deficits are funded by borrowing. The interbank market brings together suppliers of surplus short-term funds and borrowers.

If commercial banks do not use their surplus funds, the funds will sit in the account that the bank is required to maintain with the national central bank, and the funds in this account earn no interest. Lending to other banks will earn income for the bank, even though interest rates in the interbank market generally are relatively low.

Commercial banks are not allowed to have a deficit on their account with the central bank and, depending on government regulations, may be required to maintain a minimum amount on deposit at any time. A bank facing a deficit (or insufficient deposits) on any particular day must borrow to cover the shortfall. One source of funding is the interbank market.

Interbank Market

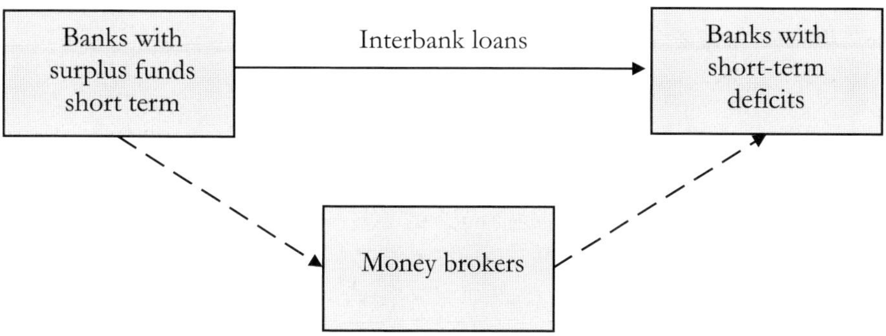

Example
Suppose there are just two banks in a country, Bank Alpha and Bank Beta. Both banks have accounts with the central bank. At the start of a particular day, both banks have $40 billion on account with the central bank. However, Bank Alpha estimates that during the day, it will have to make payments of $70 billion to Bank Beta to settle payments by its own customers to customers of Bank Beta. Therefore it forecasts a funding deficit of $30 billion for the day. To deal with this problem, it may borrow $30 billion from Bank Beta, possibly just overnight, or possibly longer if the funding deficit is expected to be long-term.

Banks can use their surplus funds in other ways, but daily interbank lending activity is substantial in volume.

Lending in the interbank market is unsecured. There is some risk that a bank to which funds are lent will fail to make the repayment of principal with interest at the end of the lending term. Interest rates therefore are lower for banks with a better credit status, and higher for other banks, although interest rates payable or receivable depend on dealing and what the parties agree on.

A role in the market has developed for intermediary banks with a very good credit status that can earn a profit by borrowing short-term at one interest rate and re-lending, perhaps for the same term, to other banks with a lower credit standing at a slightly higher rate.

Overnight and Weekend Money

Overnight money refers to money lent/borrowed before a market closing time on one day and repaid on the next banking day. The rate of interest payable on overnight money varies throughout the day, but may fall as the demand for borrowing lessens as the market nears the time for closing down, and there are still banks with surplus funds to lend. On days when money is short, however, the demand can push the interest rate up to a very high level.

Weekend money is money lent/borrowed on a Friday until the following Monday. Although Monday is the next business day, interest is payable for three days on weekend money.

Day-to-Day Money

Day-to-day money is money lent or deposited for an unspecified term, on a day-to-day basis. The lender/depositor can call back the money at any time before noon for example, and will receive same-day funds. Day-to-day money is known as money at call. Interest rates on money at call generally are more stable than overnight interest rates.

Notice Money

Notice money is money that is lent or deposited with a short notice of withdrawal, for example with two-days' or seven-days' notice of withdrawal.

Fixed Money

Funds may be lent or deposited for a fixed term, such as one week, one month, two months or three months. Interest is payable on money-market term lending at the end of the loan term, when the principal is repaid.

Intra-Day Money

In an intra-day market, money is lent and repaid within the same day, borrowing taking place in the morning and repayment in the afternoon.

Money Brokers

The function of money brokers is to act as agents or go-betweens, bringing together principals who wish to deal (borrow and lend) at mutually agreed amounts and interest rates. Brokers never act as principals themselves in any lending transaction they arrange. Their role is to intermediate between the two principals, negotiating the transaction without a requirement for direct contact between the principals, although deals arranged through money brokers are settled between the principals themselves. They are sometimes referred to as name-passing brokers, a term that suitably describes what they do, although rate passing or price passing is probably a better description.

Money brokers offer a broking service in a range of currencies and instruments, and need not confine their activities to the broking of interbank loans and deposits in domestic currency.

They are an alternative to direct dealing between the principals, and survive in business only by offering an efficient service through

- good, accurate information, and therefore access to the best available prices
- very fast execution of trades
- confidentiality. Names of the principals are passed to the counterparty only after the deal has been made, although

general descriptions of the other party, such as large German or clearer might be used during negotiations and discussing deals.

Brokers provide up-to-date indicative interest rates to the market via information providers such as Reuters. Rates are quoted for all freely convertible currencies.

Brokers charge a commission (brokerage) for their service that is based on a standard scale of charges but can be negotiable for large clients. In the US Fed-funds market, brokerage might be about $0.50 per $1 million per day. For an overnight loan of $10 million, the broker would charge about $140 at this rate to each of the principals. However an overnight loan arranged on a Friday would be for three days, until the following Monday, and the brokerage would be about $420.

Most clients of brokers are large banks, although some large non-bank corporates also deal directly with them. The broker's income is purely from commissions, and the broker is neutral in the market, simply quoting the rates available.

The London Interbank Market

London is a major money-market center. Despite its name, the London interbank market is not confined to London, and banks in other financial centers are active in the market, borrowing and lending in a variety of currencies, including sterling. The London market is supported by a worldwide network of institutions in financial centers around the world. Many investment institutions, for example, place deposits in sterling and other foreign currencies as part of their global asset-allocation policies. They might place these deposits directly in the London market with a London bank, or use a bank in another financial centre, for example their New York house bank, that also deals in London through a London-based office or a London correspondent bank. Because of very large global transfers of funds and short-term investment activity, the London market may be strongly influenced by flows of short-term money from abroad – speculative hot money.

LIBOR

Short-term loans in the interbank market are at a fixed rate for the term of the loan.

Banks that borrow or lend in the market quote indicative bid and offer prices. A bid price is the price that a bank will wish to pay on any borrowing it makes, and an offer rate is the rate that it will want to receive on any lending that it makes.

LIBOR stands for the London Interbank Offered Rate. It is the main benchmark interest rate in the London interbank market. It is most easily defined as the rate at which one bank with a high credit rating will lend to a similar bank. Since LIBOR is quoted for a number of lending terms or tenors, one month, two months, three months, six months, and one year etc., there are several LIBOR rates at any one time. Any quotation of a LIBOR rate is prefixed by its term to maturity, for example three-month LIBOR at 5.75%.

Each London bank quotes its own indicative LIBOR rate for each maturity period, but usually banks quote the same rates, with only occasional very small differences, perhaps between two and five basis points, i.e. between 0.02% and 0.05%. Occasionally, however, the spread between the rates offered by banks in the market could be as large as 12.5 basis points or even more.

Banks display their LIBOR rates on price-information screens such as Reuters, but these are indicative rates only. A time lag often occurs between a bank changing its LIBOR rate and notifying the rate change on the information system. If a bank changed its three-month LIBOR rate for example at 11.30 a.m. on Monday, price-information screens might not be altered until 11.35 a.m. In the case of banks that participate less actively in the market, its price might not be changed on its information screen until some hours later.

At one time, only banks, institutions and companies with a good credit rating could borrow from another top-rated bank at the LIBOR rate. As the London money markets developed, LIBOR has retained it status as the main benchmark rate, but highly rated banks and companies may expect to borrow short term at a rate below the LIBOR rate currently being quoted. On the other hand, those with a lesser credit rating might be offered a rate above LIBOR. Some large multinational companies can on occasion borrow short term at a rate below LIBOR in the interbank market.

Example 1
Alpha Bank is quoting a one-month LIBOR on Reuters of 6.00% per annum. Beta Bank phones and asks for a rate for borrowing $20 million for one month. If Alpha Bank does not consider Beta Bank's credit standing to be sufficiently good to offer LIBOR, it will quote a rate above its LIBOR, for example 6.125% per annum.

Example 2
A bank wishing to borrow $20 million for three months might want a rate no higher than three-month LIBOR, but preferably lower. Most banks are indicating that their current LIBOR rate is 5.75%. Its dealer could phone another bank that is quoting three-month LIBOR at 5.75%, and ask for a rate. If the bank offers 5.70%, the offer will be accepted because it is five basis points below LIBOR. If the offer had been 5.75%, it might have been accepted because the rate is LIBOR exactly. Alternatively, another bank could be approached in the hope of obtaining a lower rate.

LIBOR as a Benchmark Rate
LIBOR is the interest rate that a top-quality bank would wish to charge to another top-quality bank for an interbank loan. In practise, however, different banks will want to charge a rate of their own choice, and they will not necessarily all choose the same rate to quote, and their rates might vary throughout the day.

Indicative LIBOR rates for the London market as a whole are produced daily by the British Bankers' Association (BBA). The rate is calculated from the LIBOR rates currently being quoted at a particular time that day (11 a.m.), by a number of top London banks for different terms or tenors. The BBA LIBOR rates therefore are an average market rate.

The BBA LIBOR is a key interest rate because it is used as a guide for setting other interest rates for lending.

- Variable-rate loans provide for interest rates to be reset at regular rollover dates, often at a margin above LIBOR. For example, the interest rate on a variable-rate loan to a company might be reset every three months to 50 basis points above LIBOR as at the day before the start of the interest period. The terms of the loan agreement will specify how LIBOR should be determined. The LIBOR rate might be the BBA rate or the lending bank's own quoted LIBOR at a specific time on each reset date or the previous day.
- Other financial instruments, such as Forward-Rate Agreements (FRAs) and interest-rate swaps, often use a LIBOR rate as a reference rate. The method will be specified by which a LIBOR rate should be determined, for example as the average LIBOR rate of a panel of banks at a specified time on a specified date.
- Short-term interest-rate futures and interest-rate options use LIBOR as the interest rate payable on an underlying notional loan or deposit.

LIBID and LIMEAN

A bid rate in the interbank market is the interest rate that a bank will be prepared to pay on funds deposited with it. LIBID, or the London Interbank Bid Rate, is the rate that a London bank with good credit standing will pay on funds deposited with it by another top-rated London bank. LIBID, like LIBOR, is quoted for a number of tenors, one month, two months, three months, six months, one year and so on.

Whereas LIBOR is the rate that banks seeking to borrow in the interbank market might have to pay, LIBID is the rate that banks with surplus funds might have to accept on an interbank deposit.

LIBOR = what the indicating bank wants to RECEIVE in interest
LIBID = what the indicating bank wants to PAY in interest.

Sterling LIBID is lower than sterling LIBOR. Although the size of the spread between them can vary, especially for overnight funds, the difference usually is one-eighth of one per cent (12.5 basis points) for the same tenor of loan or deposit.

Illustrative reported rates for BBA LIBOR and BBA LIBID are shown below.

	LIBOR %	**LIBID** %	**Difference basis points**
Overnight	6 1/8	5 5/8	50.0
7 days' notice	5 3/4	5 5/8	12.5
One month	5 23/32	5 21/32	12.5
Three months	5 3/4	5 5/8	12.5
Six months	5 5/8	5 17/32	18.75
One year	5 9/16	5 7/16	12.5

The London interbank market usually is at its most active in mid-morning, when the spread between the LIBID and LIBOR rates quoted by banks generally is at its lowest for the day, possibly 6.25 basis points or one-sixteenth of one per cent. This is why the British Bankers' Association measures the daily LIBOR rate at 11 a.m.

It might seen unusual that there should be two rates, LIBOR and LIBID, because in any interbank transaction one bank is borrowing and the other is depositing funds at the same rate of interest. There cannot be two interest rates for the same transaction. Two rates are quoted, however, by banks that are active in the interbank market. To profit from taking deposits and re-lending, these banks quote a higher rate for LIBOR than LIBID.

When two top-rated banks arrange an interbank transaction, however, the interest rate that is agreed for the loan and deposit often will be somewhere between LIBOR and LIBID, and possibly the average of these two rates. Some banks therefore use LIMEAN, the average of

LIBOR and LIBID, as a reference rate for their interbank transactions.

SONIA

SONIA is another reference interest rate in the London money markets. It is an average interest rate, weighted by volume, for overnight lending in sterling on transactions made between the member firms of the Wholesale Money Brokers' Association during a particular day before 3.30 p.m.

Calculating the Interest Payable on Loans

For interbank loans and some money-market instruments, interest is payable on the loan principal or the nominal value of the instrument. Other money-market instruments are discount instruments. These include bills, and are explained in later chapters. Interest is paid at the end of the lending term, when the loan principal is repaid.

The method of calculating interest on money-market loans differs according to the currency of the loan. Interest on most currencies, including the dollar and the euro, is calculated on the assumption of a 360-day year. This means that interest payable on a loan is:

$$P \times \frac{R}{100} \times \frac{D}{360}$$

Where:

P is the loan principal
R is the annual interest rate, so that 5% = 5 and 6.76% = 6.75, etc
D is the number of calendar days in the lending period.

For some currencies, including sterling and the Australian dollar, interest is calculated on the assumption of a 365-day year, and the interest payable on a loan is:

$$P \times \frac{R}{100} \times \frac{D}{365}$$

Example
Suppose that a bank makes the following money market loans.

- €5 million for three months, from 7 June to 7 September, at 6.625% per annum
- $10 million for six months, from 30 April to 31 October, at 7.75% per annum
- $10 million for one year (365 days) at 8.0% per annum
- £10 million for three months (91 days) at 7% per annum.

What is the interest on each of these loans?

Analysis

$$\text{€5 million} \times \frac{6.625}{100} \times \frac{92}{360} = \text{€84,652.78}$$

$$\$10 \text{ million} \times \frac{7.75}{100} \times \frac{184}{360} = \$396{,}111.11$$

$$\$10 \text{ million} \times \frac{8.0}{100} \times \frac{365}{360} = \$811{,}111.11$$

$$\pounds 10 \text{ million} \times \frac{7.0}{100} \times \frac{91}{365} = \pounds 174{,}520.55$$

Notice that with the one-year loan in dollars, the interest rate is 8%, but in simple interest terms over the calendar year, the borrower pays 8.11%.

Movements in Interest Rates

Interbank interest rates fluctuate continually, but the size of the daily movement in LIBOR or LIBID normally is no more than a few basis points, either a sixteenth, one sixteenth of 1% that is 0.0625% or 6.25 basis points or an eighth, 12.50 basis points. Frequently, the closing rate at the end of the day is the same as the opening rate at the start of the day. Significant changes in LIBOR rates in the London interbank market usually are initiated by the Bank of England, whose Monetary Policy Committee uses operations in the money markets to influence the general level of short-term interest rates.

An occasional exception to the general rule that LIBOR is often fairly stable is the overnight rate, when a shortage of funds in the banking system can push up LIBOR to a much higher level until the shortage is eased. This can happen in the space of minutes early in the afternoon as the market starts to close down.

Timetable for Activity in the London Interbank Market

Banks and other institutions using the interbank market must decide each day how much they wish to borrow or lend, and for how long. Having reached their decision, they will go into the market to secure their transactions at the best rate available, often using contacts with whom they deal on a regular basis.

Market-making banks will not know at the start of each day what their volume of business will be. Their assessment of how much they might borrow or lend is continually reviewed as their market position evolves during the day. They will respond to requests for borrowing or lending from customers (banks and other market participants), but will aim to achieve some balance between borrowing and relending. They can try to achieve balance, when necessary, by changing their quoted rates for interbank lending or borrowing.

The bulk of lending and deposit activity takes place during the morning. Dealing begins as soon as the market-making banks, money brokers and lending/borrowing companies are staffed, normally from about 8 a.m. Activity peaks between 9 a.m. and 11 a.m. when banks and other institutions seek to lend or borrow at the most beneficial rates while the market is liquid and there are many potential counterparties.

After 11 a.m. activity starts to slow as an increasing number of participants withdraw from the market for the day having squared their books, i.e. borrowed the required amount of money to fund their needs for that day or lent the available surplus. If there are insufficient funds, players with a surplus will charge more to lend them to borrowers who have not yet met their funding requirements. Equally if there is a surplus of funds in the market that day, players with surplus funds at for example, 1 p.m. will have to cut their rate to find a borrower prepared to take them.

To help them manage their day-to-day funding more exactly, banks usually will expect customers with a borrowing facility to draw down any funds they require before 1 p.m. as a condition of the facility. This gives the bank time to go into the market to borrow should it need extra funds to meet the customer's requirements.

Unexpected cash flows occur nevertheless, and a bank could find that in the early afternoon there is a late deposit or withdrawal by a customer. The bank, having squared its books in the morning, would then have to seek additional funding or a place to deposit surplus funds quite late in the day. It is not unusual to see a small late flurry of activity in the market, particularly for overnight funds, around 3 p.m., immediately prior to the close of the day's trading.

For example, a bank expecting surplus funds could decide early in the day to lend much of its surplus in the interbank market for maturities ranging from seven days to six months. At 2.30 p.m., the bank's dealer might be notified of late withdrawals totalling £25 million by one of its major customers, with an instruction to borrow overnight to obtain funds to meet the withdrawal. The dealer would then telephone as many contacts as necessary in search of a willing lender at an acceptable rate.

The London Interbank Market: Conclusion

Smaller non-bank companies do not have direct access to the dealing rooms of the market-making banks, and cannot participate directly in the London interbank market. However, they do have access through their liaison officer at the bank. Companies with sufficient funds to invest short term can ask a bank to arrange a purchase of a money-market instrument such as CD on their behalf, or to deposit funds short term at a money-market rate linked to LIBID or LIBOR. A company often will use its relationship bank for placing deposits in the money market. Similarly, companies might be able to arrange a facility for borrowing short term from their bank at a rate linked to LIBOR when the funds are drawn down.

The Interbank Market in the US: Fed Funds

The central banking system in the US is the Federal Reserve System. The country is divided into 12 districts, each with its own Federal Reserve Bank. The system is supervised from Washington by the Federal Reserve Board of Governors.

Banks and other depository institutions such as savings and loan associations, are required to keep an account at their district Federal Reserve Bank. The money held on deposit at the Fed earns no interest, but banks and depository institutions are required by law to maintain a minimum amount on deposit. Minimum deposit requirements are recalculated every two weeks. The money held on deposit is known as Fed funds.

Because the deposits do not earn interest, it is undesirable for a bank to keep more than the minimum requirement on deposit. Many banks, however, have more than their minimum on deposit, whereas other banks have a shortage of funds for the business they want to conduct. An interbank market, known as the Fed funds market, therefore has developed in lending and borrowing these funds. Most lending in the market is overnight.

Fed Wire
The Fed funds market gives rise to a large number of funds transfers between banks across the US each day. The transfers are made by the same-day electronic-funds transfer system between the district Federal banks, known as the Fed wire.

Note
The Fed wire is used to settle interbank transactions in Fed funds that are dollar deposits with Federal District Banks in the US. Transactions in

eurodollars, however, are settled through the CHIPS system of the New York Clearing House. CHIPS stands for the Clearing House Interbank Payments System. Eurodollar loan transactions are loans involving dollar deposits with banks outside the US. These transactions have to be settled at banks in the US.

Running a Fed Funds Desk

Banks in the US run a Fed funds desk. The desk manager is responsible for making sure that the bank maintains sufficient deposits at the Fed, but not excessive deposits. This is a complex task, because the bank has to predict each day what the changes in its Fed funds balance will be. A reduction in the bank deposits of its customers on any day, for example, will reduce its deposits at the Fed.

Much dealing in Fed funds is direct between banks. Smaller banks with a regular surplus of deposits may have a regular daily arrangement with a larger bank to lend all its surplus Fed funds to the larger bank, with an agreement on how the interest rate should be determined. Some deals are arranged through money brokers.

Fed funds are immediately available, i.e. same-day funds, and the lending is unsecured. However, the perceived risk is fairly low, and the interest rate is comparatively low. Banks that borrow regularly in the Fed funds market therefore obtain funding at a relatively low cost. Banks that lend are exposed to some credit risk, but not much, and are at least able to earn some interest rather than earning no interest, by keeping the funds on deposit with the district Fed.

Conclusion

The interbank market is central to money-market activities and to the commercial banking system in all the major financial centers. Interest rates in this market provide a benchmark for many other short-term interest rates. Most of the other money markets have developed as alternatives to the interbank market for borrowing and lending short term.

Eurocurrency Markets

Eurocurrency markets or euromarkets are markets for borrowing and lending currencies outside their country of origin. A eurodollar, for example, is created when the owner of a dollar deposit with a bank in the US transfers the money to an account with a bank outside the US. These deposits are lent to other customers by the bank, creating eurodollar market activity.

A eurocurrency deposit has two essential characteristics.

- The organization accepting the deposit must be a bank.
- The bank receiving the deposit must be resident outside the country of origin of the currency.

For example, dollars deposited with a bank in London are eurodollars, regardless of whether the depositor resides inside or outside the US.

History of the Eurocurrency Market

Until the late 1950s, dollars deposited with banks outside the US were quickly repatriated because the banks taking the deposits invested the money in US money markets. From the late 1950s, however, as the dollar superseded sterling as the main international trading currency, the *demand* for dollar loans by non-US residents increased. Dollars deposited in Europe increasingly were lent to borrowers in Europe, and the eurodollar market emerged. The *supply* of eurodollars was increased by a US balance of trade deficit in the late 1950s and early 1960s that created a flow of dollars into the hands of non-US residents. Interest rates on eurodollars were sufficiently high to dissuade banks from investing them in US money markets.

The euromarkets were further boosted in the 1960s and 1970s by domestic banking restrictions, particularly in the US, resulting in

- increasing demand for eurodollars from the European subsidiaries of US corporations that were unable to borrow dollars in the US
- higher interest rates on eurodollars than on domestic dollar deposits. US banks used their European branches to move dollars into the euromarket, thereby circumventing restrictive US domestic-banking regulations.

Although restrictive regulations in the US were eased in the early 1970s, the eurodollar market was sufficiently well-established by then to survive and compete with the domestic US markets. In the 1970s, the eurodollar market played a key role in recycling the petrodollars of oil producing countries, lending dollars to countries suffering a balance-of-payments deficit as a consequence of the large increase in oil prices at that time.

Although euromarkets originated with the eurodollar, and the eurodollar remains the most heavily traded currency, there are markets for other eurocurrencies such as euros, sterling, yen and Swiss francs, and eurocurrency deposits and loans may be referred to as eurosterling, euroyen or euroswiss and so on.

The eurodollar market was created by the overseas offices of US banks, but banks from other countries have since joined in, particularly European, Japanese and Canadian banks. Major euromarket centres operate in London, Luxembourg, Singapore, Hong Kong, Bahrain and Nassau.

Interest Rates and Eurocurrency Market Lending

The euromarkets grew originally because of lack of regulation and price. Investors could get high interest rates on eurocurrency deposits, but borrowers also could obtain loans at a cheaper rate than in domestic markets. The narrower spread between banks' bid and offer rates for eurocurrency compared with domestic currency was due at the time to higher banking costs in the heavily regulated domestic-banking systems.

Interest rates in the euromarkets are now comparable with domestic lending and borrowing rates. If eurocurrency rates on the dollar were higher than interest rates in the US money markets, dollars from the US would be deposited in eurocurrency markets, i.e. with banks outside the US. Similarly, if eurocurrency rates on the dollar were higher than domestic money-market rates in the US, dollars would flow back to the US.

LIBOR

London is an important center for the eurocurrency market, and many big London banks are very active in the market. The interest rates quoted by banks in London therefore are considered to provide a benchmark for most currencies, and there are LIBOR rates in a variety of currencies.

As with sterling LIBOR, rates quoted by banks differ, and may vary through the day. However, a daily benchmark rate is compiled by the British Bankers' Association from an average of rates currently being quoted by top London banks.

A London bank might quote prices on screen-based information systems as follows:

1046	ALPHA BANK PLC					
	EUROCURRENCY DEPOSITS					
	14/02/01		14/02/01		14/02/01	
	$		€		£	
1M	5 5/8	5 17/32	4 27/32	4 7/8	5 23/32	5 21/32
2M	5 1/2	5 1/4	4 13/16	4 3/4	5 23/32	5 21/32
3M	5 7/16	5 11/32	4 25/32	4 11/16	5 3/4	5 5/8
6M	5 5/16	5 3/16	4 21/32	4 5/8	5 5/8	5 17/32
9M	5 1/4	5 5/32	4 21/32	4 9/16	5 9/16	5 1/2
12M	5 7/32	5 5/32	4 21/32	4 17/32	5 9/16	5 7/16

Other Quoted Interest Rates: Euribor

A feature of eurocurrency LIBOR rates is that they are rates quoted for eurocurrency loans and deposits in London, a major eurocurrency center. Other financial centers have their own interbank rates for their domestic markets. TIBOR, for example, is the Tokyo Interbank Offered Rate.

However, a different benchmark rate is used by the international markets for the euro. A benchmark rate, similar in concept to the LIBOR rates produced by the British Bankers' Association in London, is produced by the European Banking Federation in Brussels. This rate, called euribor, is compiled from offered rates of commercial banks in the euro zone countries, for loans in euros. The BBA compiles a euro LIBOR rate from rates quoted by London banks, but the euribor rate is more widely-accepted as the standard reference or benchmark for the market.

Euromarkets and the FX Markets

The euromarkets are for borrowing and lending currencies, whereas the FX markets are for buying and selling them. However there is a very close connection between the two markets.

- The difference between spot rates of exchange and forward rates of exchange in the FX markets are accounted for by the interest-rate differentials between the currencies in the euromarkets.
- There is little difference between a eurocurrency loan and a forward swap in the FX markets. A forward swap is an agreement to buy one currency in exchange for a second currency and a simultaneous agreement to sell back the currency at a future date, but at a different rate of exchange. The difference between the exchange rate for the initial purchase and subsequent sell-back is accounted for by the interest-rate differential between the eurocurrencies for the term between the two transactions.

Example
A bank wishes to buy \$10 million in three months in exchange for sterling. The current spot rate of exchange is £1 = \$1.4000, and the rate for a forward exchange contract to buy the dollars in three months is £1 = \$1.4043. Sterling can be deposited in the eurocurrency markets at 5.25% per annum and eurodollars at 6.50% per annum.

Analysis
The bank could arrange to buy the dollars immediately at a forward rate of \$1.4043, and the cost in three months would be £7,120,895 (10 million ÷ 1.4043).

To pay this sterling amount in three months, the bank could set aside some money on deposit. At an interest rate of 5.25% per annum or approximately 1.3125% per quarter, the amount that it would have to deposit to earn £7,120,895 after three months would be £7,028,644 (£ ÷ 1.013125).

The bank could, as an alternative, buy dollars and put them on deposit for three months. To have \$10 million in three months, the amount of dollars that would have to be deposited for three months at 6.5% per annum, approximately 1.625% per quarter, is \$9,840,098 (\$10 million ÷ 1.01625). At a spot rate of \$1.4000, these dollars would cost £7,028,641 to buy now.

Summary
To buy \$10 million in three months, a bank could do either of the following.

- Arrange a forward contract. Put sterling on deposit now to have £10 million after three months to buy the dollars at the forward rate. Cost in sterling now: £7,028,642.
- By dollars now and put them on deposit to have \$10 million in three months' time. Cost in sterling now £7,028,642.

Both approaches for obtaining \$10 million in three months have the same current cost, allowing for small rounding differences, indicating the close connection between the FX markets (spot and forward) and the eurocurrency markets.

Banks that trade currencies in the FX markets also will borrow and lend eurocurrencies.

Short Dates

Spot transactions in the FX markets are made on one day but not settled until two working days later, on T + 2. For example, a bank buying dollars spot in exchange for sterling on Monday will settle the transaction on Wednesday, paying sterling to the counterparty and receiving dollars in exchange, at the agreed rate of exchange. Similarly, for most eurocurrency loans, the loan period does not begin until two days after the day on which the loan is arranged.

Some transactions, in both eurocurrency lending and FX swaps, have one or more settlement dates before T + 2. These are known as short-dated transactions.

There are some regular short dates that commonly are quoted in eurocurrency market dealings. In the eurocurrency markets:

- overnight means a loan or deposit from today until tomorrow, i.e. with the loan funds delivered on the same day as the transaction and repaid the following day, one day before spot settlement on T + 2
- tom-next means a loan or deposit from tomorrow to the next day. Tomorrow means the next working day, T + 1, and next means the day after that, T + 2.

The same terminology is used in the FX markets for FX swaps. An FX swap consists of two transactions, negotiated simultaneously. One transaction may be to sell a quantity of one currency in exchange for another at an agreed exchange rate, for settlement on one date. The second transaction would then be to buy the same quantity of currency back, for settlement at a later date, but at a different rate of exchange. The difference between the exchange rate in each of the two legs of the

FX swap are calculated on the basis of the interest-rate differences between the two currencies. Thus the term tom-next is used in both the eurocurrency markets and the FX markets.

Who Uses the Eurocurrency Markets?

The FX markets and eurocurrency markets are used extensively for interbank trading, and perform the same function for foreign currencies as the interbank market for domestic currency. Banks can use the euromarkets to borrow when they are short in a currency and lend when they are long.

Banks sometimes deposit funds with another bank rather than provide them as a loan. Eurocurrency deposited by one bank with another is called a placement, and the transactions for making and withdrawing placements form what is sometimes called the placements market.

Other financial institutions and large companies also deal direct in the market. The functioning of the market is aided by the availability of current price information from information suppliers such as Reuters.

Smaller non-bank companies without direct dealing facilities also are able to participate indirectly in the eurocurrency markets, albeit at less favorable interest rates. There is widespread use of the euromarkets for:

- currency borrowing, and
- maintaining foreign-currency bank accounts.

Eurocurrency bank facilities are invaluable for managing a continuous stream of two-way cash flows in the particular currency. Cash receipts and payments in a currency rarely coincide, and currency bank accounts allow companies to place temporary surpluses on deposit or to finance temporary shortages with a line-of-credit facility.

Daily Timetable

As in the interbank market, banks try to anticipate their receipts and payments in each currency, and plan their borrowing and lending accordingly. An assessment of the position for the current day is made each morning. Customers with a eurocurrency borrowing facility are required to draw down any funds they want for the day by no later than mid-morning, enabling banks to prepare a forecast of the day's cash position by that time. They can then go into the market to borrow or lend, to square their books for the day.

Summary

The euromarkets developed rapidly because they were unregulated, and more favorable interest rates could be offered to both borrowers and lenders. The situation now is quite different. Domestic banking is less restricted than in the past, whereas the euromarkets are regulated by central banking authorities. The central banks apply regulations within their own country, but there is a large degree of international co-operation, for example in formulating capital adequacy requirements for all international banks.

With the huge expansion in international trade since the 1970s, the euromarkets no longer need to offer less regulation and better prices because they can now offer convenience. For international companies paying and receiving a variety of different currencies, it is often more convenient to borrow or deposit funds in the euromarkets instead of dealing with banks located in the country of origin of the currency.

Treasury Bills, Bank Bills and Trade Bills

General Characteristics of Bills

A bill is a form of undertaking to pay a specific amount of money at a future date, that might be up to twelve months hence. Bills can be categorized according to who has given the undertaking to pay.

- Treasury bills are issued by the treasury department of a national government, and are IOUs of the government. The term Treasury bill is used in the US and the UK. Other governments give their bills different names. French government bills, for example, are called Bons du Trésor Negotiables (BTNs).
- Bank bills are issued by a bank.
- Trade bills are issued by a commercial company, as a promise to pay a trade debt. Trade bills might be used for international trade transactions.

Because a bill is an undertaking to pay a stated amount of money at a future date up to one year, it is a form of short-term finance for the debtor. The bill holder gives credit to the debtor organization.

Treasury bills differ from bank bills and trade bills in the way they are issued.

- Treasury bills are issued by a government as a promise to pay (an IOU).
- Bank bills and trade bills are drawn by the person who will be paid, and accepted by the person who will make the payment. When it is accepted, a bill then becomes a promise to pay, an IOU.

At one time, all Treasury bills were issued in paper form on special security paper, and as bearer instruments. A bearer instrument is one giving its holder the rights of ownership. There is no requirement to register the change of ownership, so that ownership is transferred simply by giving the bill to someone else. In the US, Treasury bills are issued in electronic form, and are held by investors as entries in a computerized securities account. There are plans to dematerialize UK Treasury bills and many bank bills and for investors to hold their bills as book entries in Crest, the UK central securities depository.

Bills can be sold in the money market for bills at any time before their maturity. The seller of a bill gives up the right to eventual payment, in return for an immediate payment from the bill buyer. The purchaser of a bill acquires the right to eventual payment at maturity.

A common feature of the secondary market for all types of bill is that the market price of a bill is always less than the eventual amount payable on the bill at maturity. For example, the secondary market price of a £1,000 bill will be less than £1,000. Bills are traded at a discount to face value, and therefore are a form of discount instrument.

A bill is a form of short-term investment for its buyer. The difference between the secondary market price for a bill and the eventual payment due to the bill holder at maturity, i.e. the amount of the discount, represents interest for the investor (bill holder) in the period to maturity of the bill.

There is an active secondary market in bills, particularly government bills and bank bills. However, there are also financial institutions prepared to purchase trade bills.

Treasury Bills

Treasury bills are issued by a government to finance short-term cash shortages for its spending programme. In the US they are issued mostly for a term of 91 days (13 weeks, or three months), but some bills are issued with maturities of six months (26 weeks, or 182 days) and one year (26 weeks, or 364 days). In the UK, most Treasury bills have a maturity of 91 days, although bills occasionally are issued with a tenor of 182 days. UK Treasury bills are mainly denominated in sterling, although there are occasional issues of euro-denominated bills.

At maturity, the bill holder receives the full face value of the bill in payment from the government, without interest.

Issues of Treasury bills: weekly tender

In the US, bills are issued each week by the US Treasury department on behalf of the government, in electronic form.

Similarly, there is a weekly Treasury bill tender in the UK. At one time, bills were issued for the government by the Bank of England, and specialist financial institutions, known as discount houses, underwrote the entire issue. These arrangements no longer apply. Treasury bills are now issued weekly by the Debt Management Office, an executive agency of the Treasury.

Details of weekly Treasury bill tenders are published in the financial press, and can be found in the UK on the web site of the Debt Management Office dmo.gov.uk. An example of a weekly tender might be as follows:

Weekly Treasury bill tender

	Feb 7
Bills on offer	£100 million
Total applied for	£428 million
Total allotted	£100 million
Minimum accepted bid	98.630
Top accepted rate	5.4951%
Average rate of discount	5.4710%
Average yield	5.5467%

Bills are allotted in full to bidders at the highest price, working down to lower prices tendered until the issue is sold in full. Bills therefore are sold at differing prices, so that the tender is a form of American auction. In the example above, £100 million of 91-day bills were offered to the market. The minimum accepted price was £98.630 per £100 nominal value of bills, although not all bills were sold at this price. Some were sold for a higher price, and the top accepted rate gave the buyers of bills at this price a discount yield of 5.4951% per annum. The average yield obtained by buyers of the bills was higher at 5.5467%, because payers of the top price for the bills earn the lowest yield on their investment.

The mathematics of discounts and discount yields are explained later. In the above example, however, the minimum accepted bid was at a price of 98.63 that means the discount per £100 nominal value of bills was 1.37. As an annual percentage, the rate of discount therefore is:

$$\left[\frac{1.37}{100} \times \frac{365 \text{ days}}{91 \text{ days}}\right] = 5.4951\%$$

This is shown in the table as the top accepted rate.

The average rate of discount was 5.4710%. This represents an average purchase price for the bills of:

$$100 - \left[5.4710 \times \frac{91}{365}\right] = 98.636$$

The average yield to investors who hold on to the bills for the 91 days to maturity, is based on a return or profit of 1.364 (100 – 98.636) on the original investment of 98.636. The average yield therefore is:

$$\frac{(100 - 98.636)}{98.636} \times \frac{365}{91} \times 100\% = 5.5467\%$$

Treasury bills can be held until maturity by their original buyer, when they will be redeemed by the government at face value. Alternatively, the bills can be sold in the secondary-bills market before maturity. The secondary market value of the bills will depend on current short-term interest rates in the market, and the remaining term to maturity of the bill when it is sold. However, the market price of a bill will never exceed its face value, and the market price will move towards its face value as maturity approaches and the discount will therefore shrink to zero at maturity.

Bills of Exchange

Bank bills and trade bills or commercial bills might be referred to as bills of exchange. They differ from government bills in the way they are issued and become promises to pay.

A bill of exchange is an unconditional order in writing from one person to another, requiring the person to whom it is addressed to pay a specified sum of money on demand (sight bill) or at a future date (term bill). In the bills market, all bills are term bills.

Term bills of exchange have the following features.

- Their term to maturity, when first drawn, may be from two weeks to six months.
- They can be denominated in any currency.
- Although bills may be drawn in any currency, bills denominated in sterling or euros are more easily tradable in the London market.

Definitions
A bill is drawn on the person who is being ordered to pay.

- The drawer is the party to the bill who orders payment of the money.
- The drawee is the party owing the money to whom the bill is addressed.

Payment by Bill of Exchange

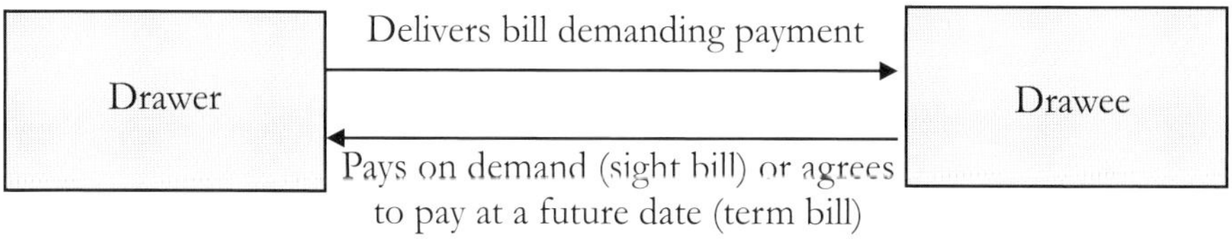

The date of the bill normally is the date when it is signed by the drawer. The place of drawing, that might be shown just as a town or city name, is also included.

There are three ways of specifying the due date for payment of a term bill:

- payment to be on a stated date
- payment to be a stated period after sight, sighting date is when the drawee signs his acceptance of the bill
- payment to be a stated period after the date of the bill.

A bill is a unconditional order to pay. It specifies the name of the payee, that might be the drawer (Pay...to our order) or a third party (Pay ...to XYZ Limited or order ...).

For a term bill with a future payment date, the drawee signs his acceptance of the order to pay (*accepts the bill*) and returns the bill to the drawer or the drawer's bank. When a bill is accepted, it becomes an IOU or promise to pay. Acceptance of a term bill is by signature across the front of the bill. To an accepted bill there also will be added details of where the payment will be made. For example an accepted bill might have wording such as Accepted payable at Epsilon Bank, Moorgate, London, for and on behalf of Omega Tango Limited, followed by the signature of an authorized person.

An example of an accepted trade bill is shown overleaf. The name of the drawee is shown in the example on the bottom left-hand side of the bill.

Bill of Exchange (Trade Bill)

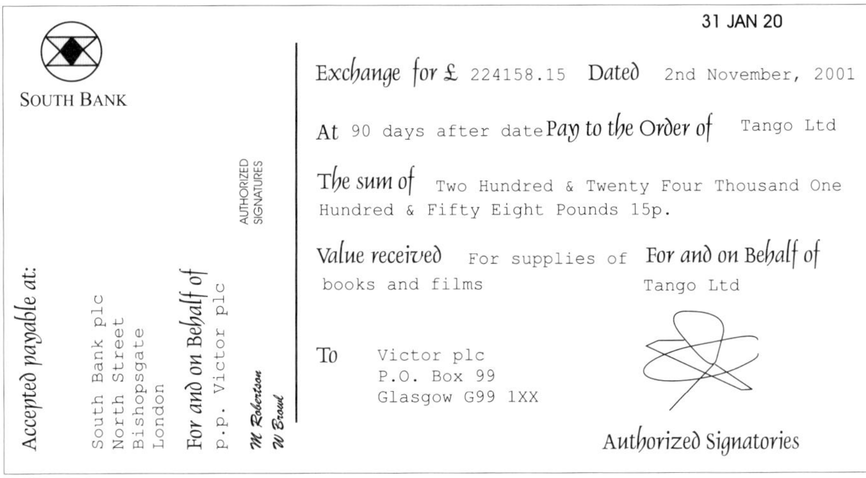
31 JAN 20

SOUTH BANK

Exchange for £ 224158.15 Dated 2nd November, 2001

At 90 days after date Pay to the Order of Tango Ltd

The sum of Two Hundred & Twenty Four Thousand One Hundred & Fifty Eight Pounds 15p.

Value received For supplies of books and films

For and on Behalf of Tango Ltd

To Victor plc
P.O. Box 99
Glasgow G99 1XX

Authorized Signatories

Accepted payable at:
South Bank plc
North Street
Bishopsgate
London

For and on Behalf of
p.p. Victor plc

AUTHORIZED SIGNATURES
M Robertson
W Broad

Discounting Bills

As an IOU, an accepted bill of exchange is a form of debt, with the drawer giving credit to the drawee. The drawer can hold on to the bill until maturity, then present it to the specified bank for payment. Alternatively, the bill holder can sell the bill before maturity for an amount below its payment value at a discount. The purchaser of the bill would then be entitled to payment at maturity.

A bill of exchange, in paper form, can be transferred by a simple endorsement. An authorized signatory of the drawer or bill holder signs the back of the bill, and gives the bill to the buyer. The buyer, as the new bill holder, will claim payment at maturity, unless the bill is sold on again.

The discount market is a market for trading in short-term debt.

- The drawee of a bill is given time to pay, i.e. credit, by the drawer of the bill, the bill holder. A bill therefore represents a debt owed by one person to another.
- A bill holder can obtain immediate finance by discounting the bill, i.e. selling the bill at a discount and receiving cash immediately in the discount market.

The ability of a bill holder to sell the bill for a reasonable price depends on the credit quality of the drawee and on the existence of a liquid secondary market in bills. This is provided by banks and other institutions dealing in the money market.

The buyer of a bill expects to make a profit by purchasing the bill at a discount to its face value and then either receiving full payment at maturity on presenting the bill for payment, or reselling the bill before maturity. The profit from buying a bill therefore represents an interest yield on a short-term investment (to maturity of the bill).

The drawer obtains immediate cash from the buyer of the bill, but in effect is borrowing short-term funds, with the interest rate for borrowing built into the discount price.

Bills are purchased extensively as a short-term investment by banks and non-banking institutions, and market dealers in bills are able to operate a liquid two-way market for accepted term bills.

Trade Bills

Trade bills are bills drawn by one non-bank company on another company, typically demanding payment for a trade debt. The ability of the drawer (bill holder) to discount a trade bill before maturity, i.e. resell the bill at a discount, depends on the financial status of the two companies concerned. Financial institutions will buy only the finest trade bills in the market, where both companies have a high credit standing.

Bank Bills

Bank bills are bills of exchange drawn on and payable by a bank. A common form of bank bill is a banker's acceptance (BA), whereby a bank accepts a bill on behalf of a customer, and promises to pay the bill at maturity. A customer might arrange an acceptance credit facility with its bank whereby the bank agrees to accept a bill, or a number of bills up to an agreed facility limit. An example of a bank bill in paper form is shown overleaf.

Bill of Exchange (Bank Bill)

Accepted 17th April 2001
Payable at Lloyds Bank Plc
Faryners House
25 Monument Street, London, EC3R 8BQ
Sorting Code No: 30-15-57T
For Lloyds Bank Plc
J. Smith
Authorized Signatories

43554 11.93 MMD27

Number 9999 — 15th April 2001

£ 210,625—00

On 15th July — Pay to our order

The sum of Two hundred & ten thousand, six hundred & twenty five pounds

Drawn against Sales of chemicals

Lloyds Bank Plc
Treasury Division
25 Monument Street
London, EC3R 8BQ

For and on behalf of
Alpha Beta plc
R Brown

When a bank accepts a bill, the bill is then payable at the office of the accepting bank.

Example

Alpha Ltd, a UK company, arranges to purchase goods for £1 million from Beta that asks for payment by means of a bank bill with a three-month maturity. Alpha Ltd asks its bank to agree to accept a bill on Alpha's behalf. Beta then draws a bill for £1 million on the bank that the bank accepts. At maturity, the bill is presented for payment and the bank pays the sum owed. The bank will then obtain reimbursement from Alpha for the payment to Beta.

Sterling Acceptance Credits

Sterling acceptance credits are facilities that provide for the drawing of sterling bills of exchange by a corporate customer on a bank. Once accepted by the bank, the bills are immediately discounted, i.e. sold in the discount market for bills, and the company receives the sale value of the bill less the bank's acceptance commission. An acceptance credit facility will be granted to the company by the bank up to a specified credit limit, and the company is able to draw bills on the bank up to this total limit. The advantage for the company of this arrangement is that it is able to raise short-term finance in the money market at a relatively low interest cost, using the credit standing of the bank.

Acceptance credit lines may be established as a complement to or as a substitution for normal bank overdraft facilities, and provide a company with an additional and flexible form of financing.

To provide funds efficiently under an acceptance credit arrangement, the procedures adopted usually are as follows:

- A facility is agreed between the client and the bank.
- If the bank bills were to be issued in paper form, the client would leave a supply of blank signed bills with the Treasury department of the bank in safe custody. If the bank bills are issued in electronic book-entry form, this is not necessary.
- At a time that the client wants to draw down funds under the facility, it will inform the bank. The bank will then issue the bill. If the bill is in paper form, this will require a blank bill, already signed by the client, to be filled in as to amount and maturity date, and to be accepted by the bank.
- The bank then discounts the bill, selling it in the discount market. The proceeds, less the bank's commission, are made available to the client.
- At the bill's maturity, the bill is presented to the bank for payment, and the bank pays the bill holder.
- The bank debits the client's account with the amount of the payment or arranges reimbursement by the client in another way. The bank will require the client to make the funds available by the time it is required to pay the bill.

Bank bills can be issued without an underlying trade transaction. For large companies with a continuing flow of large trade transactions, the issue of bankers acceptances does not have to be linked to specific trade transactions. They can be used to finance a portfolio of transactions on a mismatch basis. Bank bills also can be issued where the underlying transaction is a capital transaction. For small or medium-sized companies, however, a bank bill normally is limited to the amount of a *specific* identifiable trade transaction.

Example
A large multinational company regularly purchases goods on credit, and might ask its bank for an acceptance credit facility of £10 million whereby the bank will accept any bills drawn on it up to this limit, without the requirement for a specific underlying transaction for each separate bill.

Dollar Bankers' Acceptances
There is an active market in bankers' acceptances in the US. Only banks that are members of the US Federal Reserve are allowed to create acceptances. The top dealing banks are banks with high credit standing, and are referred to as prime banks. Their bills command the finest rates of discount.

Either-Or Facility
When a company arranges a banker's acceptance facility, the bank is agreeing to provide the company with short-term credit up to a certain limit. The company's credit line with the bank therefore is being used up. Acceptance credit facilities may be combined with a committed borrowing facility, whereby instead of drawing bills on the bank, perhaps because available discount rates on bills are making them an expensive form of finance, the company can opt instead to use up its credit by borrowing from the bank at a pre-arranged margin above LIBOR. The company is given the choice or either using up its credit facility by drawing bills on the bank or by borrowing. This is known as an either-or facility.

Eligible and Non-Eligible Bank Bills
Bank bills are either eligible or non-eligible. Eligibility refers to the willingness of the government or its agent to deal in the bills in the discount market. A government's open-market operations are described in a later chapter. Briefly, however, a government agency will deal

regularly in the money markets, either buying Treasury bills, bank bills and government bonds with a short term remaining to maturity, or entering repo transactions with financial institutions. The purpose of this dealing is both to ensure that the banking system has sufficient funds, and to control short-term interest rates in the economy. Eligible bank bills are bills that the government agency will agree to buy, it will not buy bills that are not eligible. Eligibility depends partly on the term to maturity when the bill is issued: the government will not buy bills with an original maturity longer than a specified number of days. Eligibility also depends on the identity of the bank: the government will only buy the bills of banks on their list of eligible banks.

Eligible bank bills, because they can be sold to the government in its open-market operations, are more highly rated, and attract smaller, finer rates of discount than non-eligible bank bills. However, a discount market exists for both eligible and non-eligible bank bills. Eligibility refers only to the government's willingness to buy them.

In the US, eligible bank bills are bills that the Federal Reserve would be willing to purchase in the bills market. Bank bills, especially eligible bank bills, generally are preferred to trade bills because

- as a general rule, a bank is likely to be a better credit risk than a trading company, and a bill drawn on a bank therefore is more likely to be paid at maturity
- bank bills, especially those accepted by a top-rated bank, can be sold at a lower rate of discount than trade bills, and so are a lower-cost source of finance than trade bills.

Discounts and Discount Yields: Discount Market Mathematics

Bills are sold and, in the case of government bills, issued at a price below their face value, and will be paid in full at maturity. An investor therefore earns a return on investments, and the size of the return depends on the size of the discount and the remaining period to the bill's maturity. The investment return of a purchaser of a bill can be measured as a discount yield.

The size of the discount is represented by the following formula, for currencies in which money-market interest is calculated on the assumption of a 360-day year.

$$D = F \left[\frac{R\,t}{360} \right]$$

Where:

- D is the discount to face value, in money terms
- F is the face value, or nominal value, of the bill
- R is the rate of discount, i.e. the discount yield. 5%, for example, would be expressed as 0.05 in the formula
- t is the remaining term to maturity of the bill, in days.

For bills denominated in currencies such as sterling, where interest is calculated on an assumed 365-day year in the money markets, the figure 365 should replace 360 in the formula.

Rearranging this formula, the sale price of a bill and, in the case of government bills, their original issue price, can be expressed as

$$\text{Price} = F - D = F \left[1 - \left(\frac{R\,t}{360} \right) \right]$$

Example 1
A bank accepts a bill drawn on it by a customer. The bill is for £5 million, and it has 91 days to maturity. A financial institution in the discount market is prepared to buy the bill at a discount rate of 6.0%.

Analysis
The discount to face value will be:

$$D = £5{,}000{,}000 \left[\frac{91 \times 0.06}{365} \right] = £74{,}794.52$$

The financial institution therefore will buy the bill for £5 million – £74,794.52 = £4,925,205.48.

The price could have been calculated using the pricing formula, as follows:

$$\text{Price} = £5{,}000{,}000 \left[1 - \left(\frac{0.06 \times 91}{365}\right)\right] = £4{,}925{,}205.48$$

Example 2
A company has drawn a bill on North Bank for $1 million, with an original maturity of 91 days that the bank accepted and discounted in the market at a discount rate of 4.7%. It was purchased by South Bank that rediscounts the bill when it has 61 days remaining to maturity, and the rate of discount obtained by South Bank is 4.5%.

Analysis
The original price paid by South Bank for the bill was:

$$\text{Price} = \$1{,}000{,}000 \left[1 - \left(\frac{0.047 \times 91}{360}\right)\right] = \$988{,}119.44$$

On rediscounting the bill 30 days later, South Bank will receive:

$$\text{Price} = \$1{,}000{,}000 \left[1 - \left(\frac{0.045 \times 61}{360}\right)\right] = \$992{,}375.00$$

The profit made by South Bank from buying and later selling the bill is $4,255.56. This represents its return over a 30-day investment period on its investment of $988,119.44. The higher resale price for the bill arises for two reasons:

- the shorter term to maturity. The market price of a bill moves towards its face value, and the discount falls in amount, as maturity approaches
- in this example, the lower rate of discount at which South Bank resells the bill, compared to the rate of discount at which it originally bought the bill.

Discount Yield

The discount yield is the return on investment made by the purchaser of a bill. The discount yield is calculated as follows:

$$\text{Yield (\%)} = \left[\frac{\text{Profit}}{\text{Cost of bill}}\right] \times \left[\frac{\text{360 or 365}}{\text{Days held}}\right]$$

Where:

- the cost of the bill is the price originally paid for the bill
- the profit is the difference between the cost of the bill and the money eventually received, either from payment of the bill at maturity or from reselling the bill before maturity
- the days held are the number of days for which the bill is held by the investor. This is the time in days between buying the bill and either maturity if the investor holds the bill until then, or the time the investor resells it
- 360 should be used in the formula for currencies where the money markets assume a 360-day year for interest, e.g. the dollar and euro, and 365 for currencies where the money markets assume a 365-day year for interest, e.g. sterling.

Example

An investor purchases £1 million of 91-day Treasury bills at a discount rate of 5%

Analysis

The discount on the bill is:

$$£1{,}000{,}000 \left[\frac{91 \times 0.05}{365}\right] = £12{,}465.75$$

The purchase price of the bill therefore is £987,534.25.

If the bill is held until maturity, the profit of the investor is equal to the original discount on the bill, and the discount yield will be:

$$\text{Yield (\%)} = \frac{£12{,}465.75}{£987{,}534.25} \times \frac{365}{91} = 5.06\%$$

Discount Yield and Money-Market Yield

A discount yield is not directly comparable to the yield earned on interest-bearing money-market instruments, such as a money-market loan.

Suppose that a bank lent £1 million for 91 days at an interest rate of 5%. The interest earned would be 5% x £1,000,000 x 91/365 = £12,465.75. This is the same amount as the discount on the bill in the example above. However, the interest is earned on an original investment of £1 million, compared to the investment of £987,534.25 by the bill holder. The bill holder's return therefore is higher, even though the discount rate of 5% and the interest rate of 5% are the same.

For a proper comparison of the return on a bill and the return on an interest-bearing money-market instrument, the return on the bill should be quoted as the discount yield. In the example above, the direct comparison of yields should be between the discount yield of 5.06% on the bill, and the yield of 5% on the loan.

Comparing Bond Yields

Investors in the financial markets will compare the yields available on different instruments. This is why it is useful to compare the discount yield on a bill with the money-market yield on an interest-bearing instrument. Investors also will compare money market yields will yields on bonds.

Comparisons are complicated by the fact that bonds pay interest every six months, whereas a bill with a maturity in excess of six months and a money-market instrument with a maturity in excess of six months do not provide the investor with the yield until maturity.

Comparing yields on bills with a maturity of less than six months with bond yields is more straightforward, but the comparison is complicated in the US by the fact that interest calculations on bonds assume there are 365 interest-earning days each year, not 360.

In the US, to convert the discount rate on a bill to the equivalent yield that would be earned by a buyer of bonds, the discount rate should be adjusted by the following factor:

$$\text{Equivalent bond yield} = \frac{365 \times R}{360 - (R\ t)}$$

Where:

R is the quoted discount rate
t is the number of days to maturity of the bill

Example
An investor is choosing between an investment in 91-day US Treasury bills, for which the discount rate is 4%, and bonds, for which the bond yield is 4.05%

To compare yields properly, we can convert the discount rate of 4% to an equivalent bond yield.

$$\text{Equivalent bond yield} = \frac{365 \times .04}{360 - (0.04 \times 91)} = 4.097\%$$

In this case, the yield on the bill is higher than the yield on the bond, even though the quoted discount rate (4%) is lower than the bond yield. To get round this problem dealers in bills are able to quote the equivalent bond yields on bills to investors.

Trading in Bills

Banks that deal regularly in bills will quote bid and offer rates for bills of a certain credit quality, e.g. Treasury bills. These are the rates at which they will buy bills and sell them. They expect to make their profit from the spread between their bid and offer rates.

Banks that invest in bills less regularly are unlikely to hold them from their issue until maturity. They are more likely to use bills as temporary investments for short-term surplus funds, and will sell the bills when they need the funds for other purposes. The return made by banks from investing in bills therefore is the profit they make on the difference between the buying and reselling prices for the bills.

Example

A bank purchases a bank bill on November 3. The bill has a face value of £1 million and a term of 91 days to maturity. It was purchased at a discount rate of 6.5% per annum. The bank re-sells the bill to another bank 20 days later.

Analysis

The purchase price of the bill was as follows:

$$\text{Price} = £1{,}000{,}000 \left[1 - \left(\frac{0.065 \times 91}{365}\right)\right] = £983{,}794.52$$

The price at which it resells the bill seven days later depends on the discount rate available in the market on November 23. As a general rule, the bank will expect to resell the bill at a lower discount rate than the rate at which it bought the bill, because the bill will be nearer to its maturity date.

Outcome 1

On November 23, the bank might resell the bill at a discount rate of 6.375%, 12.5 basis points below the rate at which it bought the bill. The sale price would be:

$$\text{Price} = £1{,}000{,}000 \left[1 - \left(\frac{0.06375 \times 71}{365}\right)\right] = £987{,}599.32$$

The bank will have made a profit of £3,804.80 (£987,599.32 – £983,794.52), on buying and reselling the bill that represents an investment yield of:

$$\text{Yield (\%)} = \frac{£3{,}804.80}{£983{,}794.52} \times \frac{365}{20} = 7.06\%$$

This yield has to exceed the bank's own cost of funds for the dealing in the bill to be sufficiently profitable.

Outcome 2

If interest rates in the market have fallen between November 3 and November 23, the bank will be able to resell the bill at a lower rate of discount. Suppose it sells the bill at a discount rate of 6.125%. The sale price would be:

$$\text{Price} = £1{,}000{,}000 \quad 1 - \left[\frac{0.06125 \times 71}{365}\right] = £988{,}085.62$$

Its profit on trading will be £4,291.10 (£988,085.62 – £983,794.52), giving a return on investment of:

$$\text{Yield (\%)} = \frac{£4{,}291.10}{£983{,}794.52} \times \frac{365}{20} = 7.96\%$$

This yield is higher than in Outcome 1 because of the finer rate of discount on reselling the bill.

Outcome 3

A rise in market interest rates between buying and reselling a bill will reduce the yield on a bill investment. Suppose in this example that interest rates rise between November 3 and November 23, and the bank is able to resell the bill only at a discount rate of 7.0%. Its sale price will be:

$$\text{Price} = £1{,}000{,}000 \quad \left[1 - \left(\frac{0.07 \times 71}{365}\right)\right] = £986{,}383.56$$

The profit on trading in the bill is now only £2,589.04 (£986,383.56 - £983,794.52), giving a yield of:

$$\text{Yield (\%)} = \frac{£2{,}589.04}{£983{,}794.52} \times \frac{365}{20} = 4.80\%$$

This yield might be insufficient to give the bank a net profit on its dealing, after taking into consideration its cost of funds.

Although the profit on buying and reselling bills is quite small on individual transactions, banks can make substantial profits by dealing in large quantities.

Same-Day Value

Banks trade bills in the discount market for same-day settlement. Consequently, a holder of bills can sell them in the market and receive payment on the same day as the sale. It follows that the buyer of bills must deliver same-day funds for the purchase. Same-day value helps to maintain the liquidity of the discount market.

Clearing and Settlement of Transactions in Bills

In the US and much of Europe, clearing and settlement of transactions in many bills and other money-market instruments (MMIs) is through an electronic book-entry system for transferring ownership, with delivery of the securities against payment. In London from 2001, most money-market instruments will be issued in electronic form, and paper instruments will become much less common.

When money-market instruments are dematerialized, more secure methods of clearing and settlement can be used.

The dematerialization of MMIs, and clearing and settlement of transactions in MMIs, is considered in more detail in a later chapter.

Certificates of Deposit (CDs)

Characteristics of Certificates of Deposit

A certificate of deposit or CD is a document issued by a bank or other savings institution relating to an amount of money that has been deposited with the issuer. The document recognizes the obligation of the issuer to pay this amount to the bearer with or without interest at a future date. The holder of a certificate therefore is entitled to the money on deposit, usually with interest, on the stated date. When CDs are issued in paper form, payment is obtained by presenting the CD on the appropriate date to a recognized bank that will present the CD for payment to the bank that issued it.

A sterling certificate of deposit is a tradable instrument issued in London by banks and UK building societies. CDs are bearer instruments. They are issued initially to the depositor of the funds with the bank, but can be resold in the discount market prior to maturity. Ownership of a paper CD passes on the physical transfer of the certificate to the buyer.

In practise, it is essential for investors to safeguard bearer instruments issued in paper form because of the risk of their physical loss. The paper instruments will be held in custody for investors by an organization, possibly a clearing house, and ownership recorded in a computerized system. Transfers of ownership then can be recorded by computer, without the need for any physical transfer of the paper instruments.

CDs and Time Deposits Compared

It might be useful to compare CDs with ordinary time deposits. Using a time deposit, an investor places a sum of money with a bank for a stated period of time and receives interest at a specified rate. At the end of the deposit period, the investor is entitled to withdraw the original sum deposited plus interest. A CD, in contrast, is a certificate for a time deposit. It is a bearer security, meaning that its holder is entitled to claim the deposit with interest at the end of the deposit period. Because it is a bearer security, a CD is negotiable and ownership of the CD and the underlying deposit is transferred by physical delivery from seller to buyer.

Issuing a CD

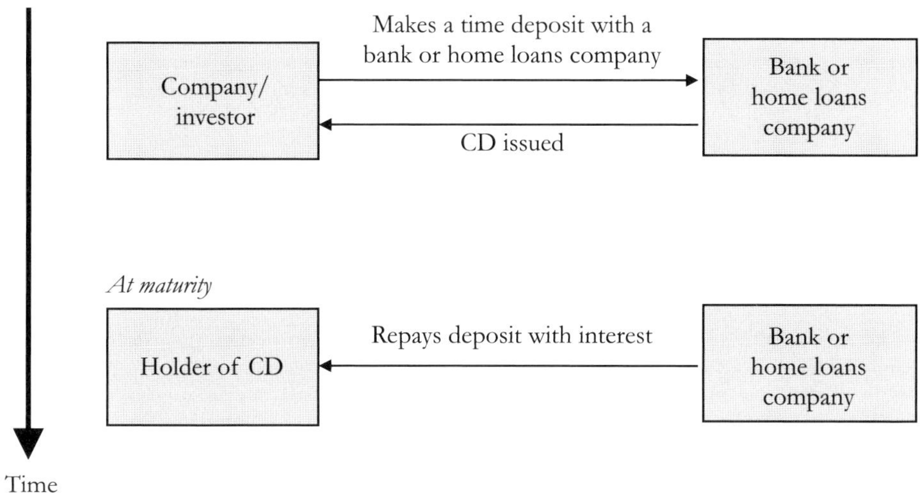

CDs have one major advantage over money-market time deposits, liquidity. A money-market deposit cannot be terminated until it matures. In contrast, CDs can be liquidated at any time at the prevailing market rate. There is a large and active secondary market in London in bank and building society CDs. Hence they are an ideal way to invest funds short term while retaining the flexibility to convert into cash at short notice if the need arises. In return for this liquidity, the investor must accept a lower yield than a money-market deposit would command. This is normally either 1/16th of 1% (6.25 basis points or 0.0625%) or 1/8th of 1% (12.5 basis points or 0.125%) below the equivalent rate for a large deposit with the same bank or building society/home-loans company.

Issue Price and Interest Yield

CDs are issued at par on an interest-to-maturity basis, for any period between 28 days and five years. Most are for a term of up to six months. For example, a CD could be issued for a deposit of £2 million for six months, with interest payable at 5.25% per annum.

A CD may be issued in either electronic or paper form. The issuing bank certifies that a specific sum has been deposited, and that:

- it will be payable to the bearer or owner of the CD
- through a recognized settlement system
- on a specified date
- with interest at a specified rate per annum, normally a fixed rate calculated on a 360-day basis for most currencies and a 365-day basis for sterling.

Interest is payable at maturity for CDs with a term of one year or less. Some CDs have a maturity longer than one year, and interim interest is payable on these annually. When long-term CDs are issued in paper form and an interim interest payment is made after 12 months, the payment is recorded on the reverse of the certificate.

Some CDs are for variable-rate deposits. The interest rate is reset every three or six months, according to terms of the CD.

How is a CD Originated?

CDs are wholesale money-market instruments for fairly large deposits. A CD originates with a decision by an organization with funds to arrange to place a sum of money on deposit with a bank for a fixed term and at an agreed rate of interest in return for receiving a negotiable CD for this amount.

The depositor must agree to leave the deposit with the bank until the CD matures. In principle, the depositor can hold the CD until maturity, when the bank will pay back the amount deposited plus interest. Alternatively, the depositor can sell the CD in the market sooner.

The CD Market

An important feature of CDs is that although the deposit remains with the bank or home-loans company until maturity of the CD, the deposit can be cashed in before maturity by the CD owner. The CD market has to be large and liquid to allow a CD holder to do this and receive a reasonable price from the sale.

At the same time, an advantage of CDs to the issuing bank is that the deposit will remain with it until maturity and cannot be withdrawn before then. This gives the bank some certainty about its funding position.

Negotiability of CDs

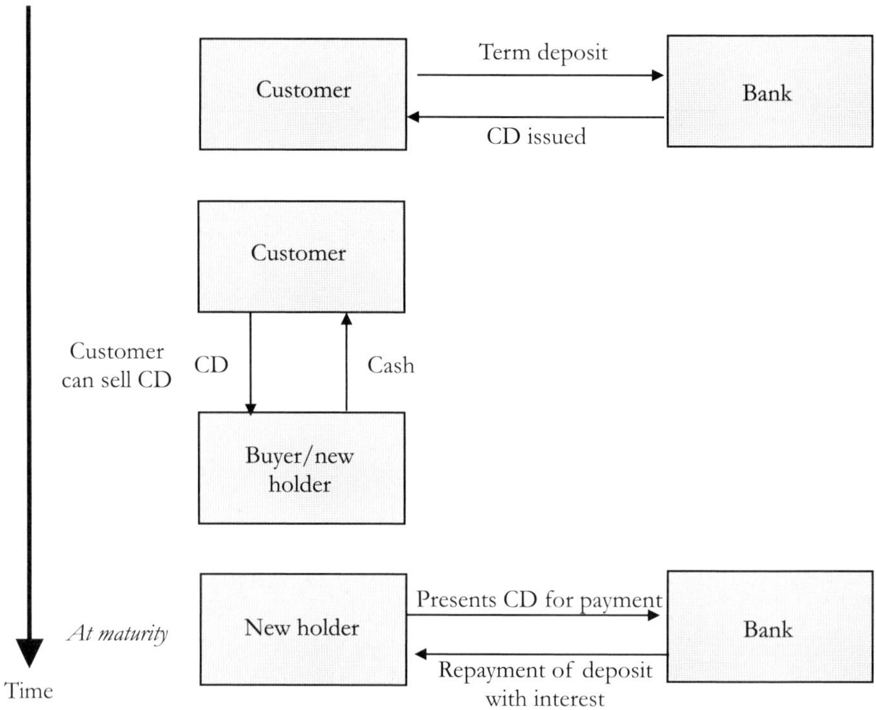

The use of CDs was developed in the UK during the 1960s. They were attractive to investors seeking high interest rates on time deposits, but who were reluctant to commit their money to the bank for the full term of the deposit. The sterling CD market was inaugurated in 1968 by financial institutions known as discount houses that specialized in money-market dealing. The discount houses were prepared to quote prices for both buying and selling CDs that are fully negotiable, and the discount houses ensured an active and liquid secondary market for sellers and buyers. Because a CD can be sold by its holder at any time, the holder has a much higher degree of liquidity than with a conventional term deposit.

Buyers of CDs in the secondary market are banks and other companies or institutions wishing to invest at money-market rates. CDs offer a competitive rate of interest to the investor, together with comparatively low credit risk, and a liquid secondary market. The risk that the bank will fail to repay the deposit with interest at maturity should be fairly small.

The CD market is relatively important to the banking system. CDs are an alternative to the interbank market for interbank money transactions, assisting with maturity matching, i.e. matching the maturity of a bank's liabilities, deposits etc., with the maturity of its assets, so that maturing assets can be used to meet the bank's obligations as its liabilities mature.

They are also an alternative to the interbank market for money transactions between banks. Instead of one bank borrowing money from another, it can sell CDs that it holds. Most CDs are held as assets (short-term investments) by banks.

CD Interest Rates

On primary issue, a customer places a term deposit with a bank and the bank issues a CD to the customer. The rate of interest payable typically will be at 1/8 of 1% (12.5 basis points) below LIBOR. The yield on a sterling CD in the secondary market typically is about 6.25 basis points to 12.5 basis points below the comparable LIBOR rate. For example, if three-month LIBOR is 5%, the rate for a three-month CD in the secondary market might be 4 15/16%.

Unlike bills, where prices are quoted as a discount rate, CD prices are on a yield-to-maturity basis. The following price formula applies:

$$P = \frac{V}{1 + \left(\frac{Y \times D}{360^{*}}\right)}$$

* 360 days for CDs in most other currencies, including dollars and euros and 365 days for sterling..

Where:

- P is the sale/purchase price of the CD
- V is the value of the deposit, the sum deposited, plus interest payable at maturity

Y is the yield required on the CD. For a yield of 5%, Y = 0.05, etc.

D is the number of days to maturity.

Example

A CD is issued for a deposit of £1 million with a term to maturity of 91 days. At the end of this term, accumulated interest will be £16,000. The money-market yield on the CD therefore will be:

$$\frac{£16{,}000}{£1{,}000{,}000} \times \frac{365}{91} \times 100\% = 6.4176\%$$

The CD was issued to Alpha that sells it in the market seven days later at an interest rate of 6.25% per annum.

The sale price will be:

$$P = \frac{£1{,}016{,}000}{1 + \left(\frac{0.0625 \times (91 - 7)}{365}\right)}$$

$$= £1{,}016{,}000 \div 1.01438$$

$$= £1{,}001{,}597.03$$

Note

The higher the yield required by the purchaser, the lower the sale price of the CD will be.

Dollar CDs

In the UK, CDs are denominated mainly in sterling, but there is a market for dollar CDs issued in London, and for CDs denominated in euros.

There is a liquid secondary market in these as well as sterling CDs. In most respects, dollar CDs and sterling CDs are similar, although dollar CDs, interest is calculated on an actual/360-day basis, rather than an actual/365 day basis.

6

Commercial Paper

As an alternative to bank borrowing, bills of exchange or Certificates of Deposit, companies can raise short-term finance by issuing commercial paper.

What is Commercial Paper?

Commercial paper (CP) is a short-term financial instrument, consisting of unsecured promissory notes issued in bearer form that can be readily traded. At maturity, the CP issuer pays the amount due to the person presenting the paper. CP is an example of securitization, i.e. raising loan funds by issuing debt securities rather than by bank borrowing. A bank acts as agent for a CP issue, packaging and selling the paper to investors, but does not advance it own funds. Securitization, such as CP, is also a form of disintermediation, i.e. raising funds directly from investors without the banks acting as intermediaries through their deposits and loans business.

CP traditionally has been issued in paper form, but also may be issued in a dematerialized form into the system of a central securities depository. This is explained further in Chapter 8. For the purpose of explaining CP in this chapter, it will be assumed that CP is in paper form.

CP is issued as a series of notes, and each note promises to pay the bearer a stated sum of money at the maturity date. Each note shows:

- the name of the issuing company
- the amount (value) of the note

- the issue date
- the maturity date
- a certificate of authentication, signed by an authorized signatory of the company's issue agent.

Each note also will indicate that it is negotiable, its bearer is entitled to payment, and that payment will be made on presentation of the note at maturity through a recognized bank by the issue agent on behalf of the company.

Maturity

CP is a short-term loan note with a maturity of between one day and 270 days in the US and between one day and 270 days elsewhere. The most common maturities on CP notes are one and three months. Similar instruments issued with a maturity from one year up to thirty years are called *medium-term notes (MTNs).*

Currency and Value

CP can be issued in any currency. The minimum value for a sterling note is £100,000, but notes can be for up to £1 million. Most CP is issued in dollars, and common note values are $100,000, $250,000 and $500,000.

When CP is issued in dematerialized form, it exists only as computer records. There are no physical notes, and investors are able to purchase CP in flexible denominations.

A CP programme can include an option to issue paper in an alternative currency. For example, a UK company might arrange a CP program for £200 million, with the option to issue paper in either sterling or dollars.

Issue Price

A CP note is a promise to pay a fixed sum (the face value) at maturity, without interest. For example, if a CP note for £500,000 is issued on 1 August and is payable three months later, the issuer will pay £500,000 at maturity on 1 November.

In this respect, commercial paper is similar to a bill of exchange, in that it is sold at a discount to its face value. The size of the discount reflects the yield to the buyer/investor.

However, not all commercial paper is discount paper. Some eurocommercial paper (ECP) has been issued as interest-bearing instruments.

CP Markets and the Role of Banks as Intermediaries

Banks do not act as guarantors for CP issued by their corporate clients. Their role in the CP market is to

- distribute new issues of CP, i.e. sell paper to investors
- act as dealers in the secondary CP market
- act as paying agents on behalf of the issuer, making the payments to the holders of the paper at maturity.

Rates offered on CP are higher than bill discount rates because CP is unsecured and the investor is exposed to credit risk, the risk that the issuer will fail to redeem the paper at maturity. Because CP is unsecured, it is now a general requirement for CP programs to be given a credit rating.

History of the CP Markets

The CP market in the US has a long history dating back to the nineteenth century. It has gone through several periods of growth, but has expanded substantially since the 1960s, particularly during the 1980s.

The commercial paper market also grew rapidly in Europe in the 1980s, when many companies found that they could borrow more cheaply in the securities/paper market than by traditional bank lending.

A consequence of the growth in the European CP market was the loosening of ties between companies and their relationship banks, as companies did business with the institutions that gave them the lowest cost of funds. Unlike the US, much of the commercial paper in Europe was placed with banks and transactional banking emerged as a lower-cost alternative to relationship banking.

The main CP markets are the following.

- The domestic US market in CP. The US commercial paper market (USCP) is the largest CP market in the world. It operates in the US and in dollar-denominated paper.
- The eurocommercial paper market (ECP). This operates from various financial centres in Europe, particularly London, with CP denominated mainly in dollars.

There are also domestic CP markets in several countries, although these are relatively small. For example, there is a sterling commercial paper market based in London.

Who Issues CP?

Commercial paper can be issued by banks, other financial institutions and companies outside the finance sector. The issuer should be sufficiently large and financially sound to justify a CP program. Funds raised from a CP issue should be for short-term seasonal or cyclical working-capital requirements.

Credit Rating

Commercial paper is unsecured, and investors must rely on the promise of the issuer to pay at maturity. Formal credit rating is required for a CP program.

The commonly used credit ratings for CP are those provided by the US agencies Moody's and Standard & Poor's (S&P). These give a credit rating to issued debt securities on request from the issuer.

Moody's Short-Term Debt Ratings

Rating	Characteristics
Prime 1	The issuer has a superior ability to repay, and assured sources of alternative liquidity. The issuer also has a leading position in a strong industry. It achieves high returns on capital employed, and a high ratio of equity finance, i.e. financial gearing is low. It has a high level of profit cover for its interest charges (high interest cover). It has strong cash generation.
Prime 2	The issuer has a strong ability to repay, with ample sources of alternative liquidity. A Prime 2 rating has similar characteristics to Prime 1 rating, but to a lesser degree. There is more variability in the rate of profit growth, and in interest cover.
Prime 3	The issuer has acceptable ability to repay and adequate sources of alternative liquidity. The issuer is more likely to be affected by changes in industry or market conditions. Variability in earnings could result in a need for relatively high borrowing levels and a high level of financial gearing or leverage.
Not Prime	Short-term debt that does not fall into any of the other three categories. Below investment grade.

Prime 1, Prime 2 and Prime 3 are all investment-grade ratings. Prime is often shortened to P. A top-rated, short-term debt issue therefore is graded P1.

Standard & Poor's Short-Term Debt Ratings

Rating	Characteristics
A-1	Highest category. The issue has strong safety characteristics. An A-1 + rating indicates *extremely* strong safety characteristics.
A-2	This rating is not as high as A-1, but the issuer still has a satisfactory capacity for timely payments.
A-3	The issuer has adequate capacity for timely payments, but there is greater vulnerable to adverse changes in circumstances than with debt rated A-1 and A-2.
B	Only speculative capacity for timely payment.
C	Doubtful capacity for payment.
D	Payment is in default.

The A-1, A-2 and A-3 grades are all investment-grade ratings. Short-term debt issues given a top-grade credit rating by both Standard & Poor's and Moody's are referred to as A1/P1 debt.

A1/P1 paper will sell at the finest rates. Some investors will be willing to buy CP that does not have an A1/P1 rating, but will expect a bigger discount on the purchase price.

A1/P1-rated CP might be placed with investors at a cost of between 10 and 25 basis points (0.10% - 0.25%) less than the cost for issuers whose paper is rated only A2/P2. The benefit of a higher rating can be quite large.

Example

A large company with occasional surplus funds to invest short term has formulated the following policy for invcsting in CP.

Its credit risks will be limited by:

- placing a maximum investing limit in the CP of any single company or bank
- specifying that the CP must have a minimum credit rating of A1/P1 for example

- investing in lower-rated paper (A2/P2) only if the yield offered is sufficiently above the yield available on higher-rated paper to compensate for the higher credit risk
- permitting some investment in unrated paper only if it has been issued by a bank or non-bank corporate of the highest credit standing.

A basic policy on CP might allow the treasury department of a large company to invest in A1/P1 rated CP with a maximum maturity of six months, and a maximum investment of, for example, $20 million in the CP of any single organization. Any proposal to invest outside these limits would be referred to the finance director or treasury committee for agreement.

How is Commercial Paper Issued?

A company or institution wishing to raise funds by issuing CP will negotiate a program with a dealer or agent or several dealers. The dealer will be a bank that specializes in CP issues.

A CP program is for a set term that can be extended by agreement and for a maximum amount. A CP program is for at least $100 million or £50 million, but programs usually are much larger than the minimum. For example, a company might arrange a two-year program with a dealer to issue CP up to a maximum value of $300 million. Within this limit, the company can issue CP notes at any time within the two years.

Issues can be for any acceptable maturity, one to 270 days in the US, seven to 364 days in the UK. A company with a £250-million program might begin by issuing £70 million of paper with a maturity of two months, and three weeks later issue a further £80 million with a maturity of three months, and then a further £100 million two weeks after that, taking the amount issued up the limit of the facility. At the end of the second month, the first £70 million issue will be redeemed, and the company could, if it wished, issue new paper for a further £70 million.

Issuers of CP have flexibility on maturities and can let out paper to the market as tap stocks, issuing only as and when they wish to, or when there is a demand in the market for CP so that interest rates are favorable.

The bank acting as agent or dealer will advise the company about laws and regulations governing CP and on selecting an appropriate time for making an issue. It also will find investors to buy the paper, and negotiate with them on price. Because CP is sold directly to investors, the issuer could obtain a lower cost of funds than by borrowing from a bank, but the price will depend on conditions in the market and the credit rating of the paper.

CP Buyers and Dealers

Purchasers of CP are mainly banks and other financial institutions and cash-rich companies looking for short-term investments. Some banks, including the dealers who arrange CP programs, act as dealers, buying and reselling CP to create a liquid secondary market.

An example of screen-based information on available secondary market CP rates is shown below. Prices (interest yields) are shown for 5-day, 15-day and 30-day USCP for issues by a variety of companies.

CP Rates: Price Information Screen

US COMMERCIAL PAPER RATES ICPB

1333

CO.	5-DAY	15	30	CO.	5-DAY	15	30
GECC	3.500	3.850	3.850	DCC	3.850	3.850	3.850
GMAC*	3.875	3.850	3.850	HFC	3.900	3.875	3.875
FMCC	3.900+	3.850	3.850	WCC	3.500	3.950	4.200
SRAC	3.850	3.850	3.850	HLR	3.500	3.850	3.875
AMX	3.850	3.850	3.850	CCC	+3.900	3.850	3.850+
ACA	3.880	3.850	3.850	BUSF	3.670	3.670	3.720
PRUD				GEFS	CLOSED	CLOSED	CLOSED
CIT	UNQ	3.700	3.700				
ITTF	3.90	3.850	3.750	CVRN	RUR	3.800	3.800
BPGRP	CLOSED	CLOSED	CLOSED	AGFC	3.880	3.850	3.850

Like bills of exchange and certificates of deposit, commercial paper needs a liquid market to be an attractive short-term investment. Buyers must be able to:

- purchase CP for any maturity at any time of their choosing, and
- resell CP before maturity if they desire.

The most liquid CP market is in the US, where there is a large market in on-shore dollars (US commercial paper or USCP). However, the secondary market for CP is not as liquid as the secondary market for certificates of deposit. Many investors buy CP on issue and hold it until maturity. In contrast, the purpose of issuing CDs is to give their holder the opportunity to sell in the secondary market before maturity.

Commercial Paper Yields and Prices

Interest on CP generally is paid in the form of issuing the paper at a discount to face value. In contrast, Medium-Term Notes with a maturity of over one year are issued in coupon form, and interest is paid at regular intervals at the coupon rate.

The price at which CP is sold can be calculated in the same way as the price of bills of exchange.

$$P = \frac{F}{\left[1 + \frac{(R \times D)}{360 \text{ or } 365^*}\right]}$$

Where:

P is the sale price
F is the face value of the CP (the amount payable at maturity)
R is the interest rate on the paper as a percentage. (4.5% = 0.045, etc.)
D is the number of days to maturity of the CP.

360 should be used in the formula for currencies for which

money-market interest is calculated on an actual/360-day basis, and 365 should be used for currencies for which interest is calculated on an actual/365-day basis.

Example

Two companies, Sierra and Tango, each issue £10 million of CP with a three-month maturity (91 days). Sierra's CP has an A1/P1 credit rating, and was issued at 6.6%. Tango's CP has a lower credit rating, and was issued at 7.5%.

Analysis

Sierra will sell its CP for the following price.

$$\frac{£10\text{ million}}{\left[1+\left(\frac{(0.066\times 91)}{365}\right)\right]}$$

$$= £10\text{ million}/1.01.01645$$

$$= £9{,}838{,}115.83$$

Tango will sell its CP for a lower price.

$$\frac{£10\text{ million}}{\left[1+\left(\frac{(0.075\times 91)}{365}\right)\right]}$$

$$= £10\text{ million}/1.01870$$

$$= £9{,}816{,}445.91$$

Investors in Tango's CP demand a higher yield to compensate them for the greater credit risk.

US Commercial Paper (USCP) Market

CP originated in the US, and the USCP market remains the world's largest CP market. Investors range from insurance companies and pension funds to corporations placing their surplus funds. US market regulators require CP programs to have two US credit ratings. By far the greatest volume of activity is for CP with A1+/P1 and A1/P1 ratings.

Issuers

Many large creditworthy US companies issue USCP, mainly to fund seasonal cash requirements at a low rate. Banks and financial institutions also use USCP as part of their funding portfolio. The major vehicle finance companies such as GE Capital tap the USCP market to fund a significant proportion of their on-going funding needs.

Investors

Investment managers in the US were using CP well in advance of their European counterparts, and CP forms a well-established part of the portfolio of many investment managers. At one time there was a significant yield premium to be gained by investing in good-quality US corporate paper rather than depositing funds with good-quality US banks, but this is no longer the case. Corporate paper bearing a particular credit rating trades at broadly the same rate as the CP of a bank with a similar credit rating. USCP issued by a bank occasionally trades at a yield below the interest rate on a deposit with the same bank, reflecting the relative liquidity of CP compared with a term deposit and the consequent preference of investors for a bank's CP over investment in a term bank deposit.

Dealers

USCP can be placed with investors either through a dealer, or several dealers, acting as an intermediary between issuer and investor, or directly by the company.

Slightly more than one half of USCP is issued through dealers. Despite the liberalization of the US securities markets allowing commercial banks to compete with the investment banks, USCP dealing is almost exclusively the preserve of large US investment banks.

Many major US corporations and finance houses with USCP programs issue direct to investors and do not place their paper through dealers. They do this by direct phone contact and by posting rates, i.e. indicating the rates at which they are prepared to issue, on screens carried by the major information services. Some of the largest programs have directly placed issues worth several billion dollars outstanding at any one time.

Investment Return and USCP

In the early 1980s the investment return on USCP exceeded dollar LIBOR for an equivalent maturity by a substantial margin of up to 200 basis points (2.00%). For example, if three-month dollar LIBOR were 7%, three-month USCP might trade at up to 9%. Yields have fallen significantly over time.

As a broad guideline, the general yield levels of the various credit-quality bands are as follows for a corporate issuer of CP:

Credit rating	Investment yield
A1+/P1	10-30 basis points below LIBOR
A1/P1	10 basis points below LIBOR to 25 basis points above LIBOR
A2/P2	Up to 150 basis points or more above LIBOR

Length of Investment

The USCP market tends to be short term with the bulk of issues being for 30 days or less, a significant amount of overnight issues and an average period to maturity of around five days. USCP can be issued for up to 270 days but few investors need to place their funds for such a long period and would demand a higher premium over dollar LIBOR than for shorter periods.

Regulation

In 1991, the Securities and Exchange Commission (SEC) reacted to tremors in the US financial markets, high default levels, the Savings and Loan industry crisis, and financial problems for many US banks by tightening up its regulations for the USCP market. Money-market funds in the US were prohibited from investing more than 5% of their assets in commercial paper below the top grade and no more than 1% in the paper of any single issuer. The effect of this new rule was to drive some lesser-rated borrowers out of the USCP market.

Eurocommercial Paper (ECP)

The eurocommercial paper market (Euro-CP or ECP market) is an international market for commercial paper outside the US. Paper may be issued in any freely convertible currency, but the market enjoyed a substantial boost with the introduction of the euro in 1999.

The constituency of ECP issuers is broadly similar to the USCP market, namely sovereign governments and sovereign-backed supranationals such as the Swedish Export Credit Agency and the European Investment Bank, banks and companies. Sovereign and sovereign-backed issues represent a greater proportion of the market than in the US. A number of US companies have established euro CP programs, to diversify their funding away from the much larger US market.

As an investment, euro CP may be seen as an alternative to equities. When returns on equities are volatile or uncertain, investors are likely to switch more of their funds into the money markets.

ECP is often issued through dealers because dealer commissions are reasonably low. However, some large issuers of ECP sell their paper direct to investors.

Investment yields on dollar ECP are now running at broadly the same levels as those available to USCP investors with differences of no more than a few basis points on any given day.

The ECP market has a much longer-term focus than the USCP market with an average maturity of around 45 days. ECP issues of 90 days or more also are common.

In addition to the international market in ECP, there are also domestic CP markets based in financial centres such as London (sterling CP), Japan and Paris. The French domestic market for CP (billets de trésorerie) is well-established.

Commercial Paper and Currency Swaps

Some banks might offer a package of CP combined with a currency swap. Such packages can be offered to either issuers of CP or investors in CP.

CP denominated in one currency can be packaged with a currency swap to produce surrogate funding in a second currency. A CP program might be arranged in dollars, for example, and there would be regular issues of CP in dollars, with interest paid in dollars to investors. The CP issuer uses the swap arrangement to:

- exchange the dollar funding for a second currency, e.g. sterling
- receive swap payments in dollars to meet interest obligations on the CP, and in return make swap payments in the second currency.

The net result is that CP is issued in dollars, but the issuer's funding and interest payments are in the second currency, in this example sterling. The arrangement is illustrated below.

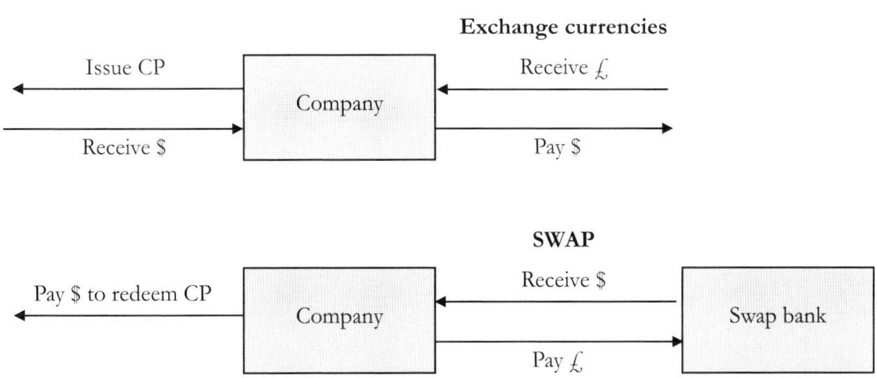

Banks also will arrange to sell CP to investors packaged with a swap. The investor arranges to invest a regular amount in the CP of a particular issuer as subsequent issues are made and redeemed. The CP will pay interest in the currency of issue, for example dollars. The swap package enables the investor to swap income in the CP currency into income in a second currency. An example is illustrated below in which an investor in USCP swaps the investment income into sterling.

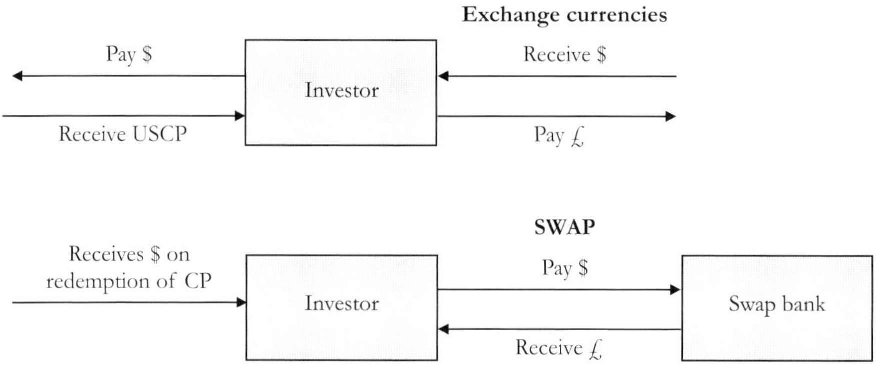

The main reason for packaging CP with a currency swap is for banks to enhance the yield to investors. For example, CP is largely dollar-denominated. The dollar may not be a currency in which a UK company or institution wishes to invest. In such circumstances a bank could combine a three-month dollar CP note with a three-month currency swap from dollars into sterling, thereby creating a surrogate sterling investment. The advantages of this arrangement are that:

- the investment is denominated in a currency in which there is investor demand, and
- the currency swap can enhance the yield.

Dematerialization of CP

CP issued in paper from is a bearer instrument, and the investor would have the responsibility for taking delivery and arranging safe custody of the bearer certificate. As this represents an additional administrative burden and cost that might deter investors, the banks evolved a system of offering safe custody free of charge to investors in primary, secondary and packaged CP.

CP lends itself fairly readily to issue in dematerialized form. A new issue of CP can be issued into the book-entry system of a central securities depository and held by investors in electronic form. For an issue of CP by the same issuer and with the same maturity date, all the paper will be fungible, and transferable within the system.

Advantages of Commercial Paper

Commercial paper and medium-term notes are flexible financial investments for the borrower, who is able to choose the period to maturity for any issue within a program. For example, a company could decide that it wants to issue some new paper at the end of April, with maturity in the middle of July. However, if the interest rates payable at the time for this borrowing term are not attractive enough, the borrower can rethink and alter the term of the issue. It might issue paper with a maturity in mid-May, for example. Corporate borrowers therefore are able to play the market and try to schedule borrowing for when they expect interest rates to be most favorable.

Other advantages of commercial paper are:

For the Issuer

- Although interest rates are determined by market conditions, companies might obtain slightly lower interest rates by issuing CP than if they borrowed directly from a bank.
- A CP programme can be arranged very quickly, within two to three weeks. However, dealers often wish to have an information circular about the issue that they can present to investors in order to generate interest in buying the paper. Consequently, a CP program might take a few weeks to prepare. Once a program is established, CP can be issued very rapidly.

The issuer will remain in regular contact with the dealer/agent about when to make a new issue, how much to issue and for what maturity.

For the Investor

- An investment in commercial paper can yield a higher return than a bank deposit, bills of exchange or CDs. Like bills and CDs, the existence of a secondhand market gives a CP investor the option to liquidate the investment at any time before maturity.

Sale and Repurchase Agreements (Repo)

What is Repo?

A sale-and-repurchase agreement (repo) is the sale of securities by a repo dealer (a bank) to a counterparty, combined with a simultaneous agreement by the repo dealer to buy back the securities at a future date at the original sale price plus interest. The debt securities used in repo transactions typically are government bills or bonds, or other very high-quality issues.

Repo Agreement

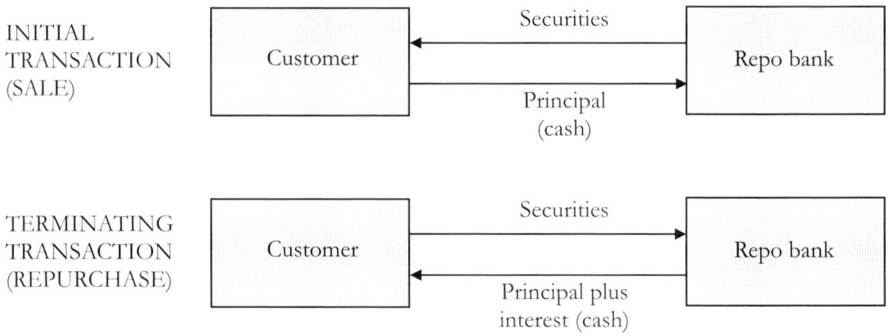

The repo market is now well-established in the major financial centers, such as the US and the European Union countries. Repos are used:

- by banks, to obtain short-term funding or to invest surplus funds short-term

- by the government (or its agency), in its open-market operations in the money markets (described in Chapter 9)
- by money-market investors
- by bond-trading houses to finance the trading inventories they hold
- by securities-markets professionals to obtain specific securities for short periods of time.

A bond-trading house might purchase part of a new issue of bonds and finance its purchase by means of a repo. The trading house will sell the bonds for future repurchase, and use the money obtained from the sale to pay for the bonds. The repurchase can be timed to coincide with the sale of the bonds to other investors by the trading house. In this way, the bonds will have been largely financed by the repo agreement between their original purchase and subsequent resale.

A bond-trading house can use repo finance to obtain a lower rate of interest on its short-term funding of its positions in government bonds. Because high-quality bonds are provided as collateral for the borrowing, the interest rate payable will be comparatively low, for example lower than for short-term unsecured borrowing.

Features of Repo Agreements

Although technically a sale of securities and their subsequent repurchase, a repo is essentially a short-term secured loan with the collateral provided by the securities. The seller of the securities receives funds from the buyer, and provides collateral in the form of the securities. When the loan is repaid at maturity, the securities providing the collateral are returned.

Many repo transactions are made between banks. Whereas an interbank loan is an unsecured short-term loan, a repo is a secured short-term loan.

Repo transactions are unusual in that they involve a sale and purchase of securities such as bonds, but their purpose is not the same as an outright sale or purchase. They are temporary deals that will unwind in a short time. Most repo trades are very short term, the repurchase date typically being one week or two weeks after the original sale date. In the US, the most common trade is overnight, but this is less common in Europe. The repurchase date need not be specified, and the end date in an agreement may be left open. The parties agree on the pricing, valuation and risk-reduction methods to be used while the deal remains open.

Securities provided as collateral often will be in the same currency as the loan, but this need not be the case. The Bank of England, for example, will accept some euro-denominated securities as collateral, for example euro-denominated bonds or bills issued by the UK government or other governments of countries in the European Economic Area.

There are several key elements in a repo agreement.

Suppose that Omega Bank would like to borrow funds by means of a repo transaction. It has investments in bonds that it is prepared to provide as collateral. Another bank, Delta Bank, might be willing to be the counterparty in a repo transaction. The details that Omega Bank and Delta Bank would have to agree would include:

- which of the securities held by Omega Bank would be acceptable to Delta Bank as collateral
- how these securities should be valued, and what price Delta Bank would be prepared to pay for them, i.e. how much Delta Bank would be willing to lend against the securities as collateral
- what the term of the loan should be, i.e. what the sale and repurchase dates should be
- what the repurchase price will be, i.e. what the interest rate for the loan should be.

Margin (Haircut)

Securities provided as collateral may fall in value during the term of the agreement. For example, suppose that Alpha Bank and Beta Bank arrange a repo whereby Alpha sells government bonds valued at $20 million to Beta, and Beta lends $20 million to Alpha against the security of these bonds for a period of two weeks. During the two-week period, the bonds may fall in value, perhaps to $19.75 million. If this were to happen, the security held by Beta Bank would be less in value than the amount of the loan, and so some of the loan ($250,000) would be unsecured. Because repo is meant to be a secured loan arrangement, this situation would be unacceptable to Beta.

The possibility of a fall in securities prices during the term of a repo is dealt with in two ways.

- The borrower is required to provide securities as collateral with a market value in excess of the amount of money borrowed. The difference between the market value of the securities provided and the amount of money lent is known as margin, and sometimes as a haircut.
- If the securities fall in value to the point where their current market value is lower than the amount of funds lent, the borrower is required to provide additional securities with a market value sufficient to make up the deficit. Extra securities provided as margin in this way are referred to, not surprisingly, as additional margin.

The size of the margin or haircut may depend on the credit quality of the securities provided as collateral, and their remaining term to maturity. Bonds with a short remaining term to maturity are much less price-volatile than bonds with a longer remaining term to maturity, and the margin on these bonds therefore will be less.

The size of a haircut also may vary with the term to maturity of the repo. For a repo with a one-week term, the haircut for US Treasury bills might be just 10 basis points (0.10%). For home loan-backed securities, a haircut of about 2% (200 basis points) might be required for a one-week repo. For a three-month repo, the haircut for Treasury bills might be as high as 75 basis points (0.75%).

Example
Alpha Bank borrows $20 million from Beta Bank for one week under a repo agreement. Alpha is required to provide government bonds as collateral to the value (as at the start of the agreement) of $20.2 million.

Midway through the term of the repo, a rise in market interest rates sends the market value of the bonds down, from $20.4 million to $19.75 million. Under the terms of the repo agreement, Alpha will be required to provide additional margin. Because the difference between the money lent ($20 million) and the securities held as collateral ($19.75 million) is $250,000, Alpha will be required to provide securities with a value of $250,000 plus a margin of perhaps $255,000.

Documentation

As the markets developed, the contractual arrangements and documentation for repo agreements became largely standardized. Parties that deal with each other regularly are likely to use a Master Agreement. For example, government agencies that deal in repo in their open-market operations use a standard agreement for transactions with all counterparties. A Master Agreement sets out the contractual arrangements for all subsequent repo transactions between the parties, and individual transactions as they are struck, are added as appendices to the Master Agreement.

- For repo in dollars, a standard Master Agreement has been produced by the Public Securities Association (PSA).
- For non-dollar repo, the PSA and ISMA have produced a PSA/ISMA Global Master Repurchase Agreement.

Items covered by a Master Agreement will be all the terms and conditions applying to every transaction, such as:

- the identity of the two parties
- ownership of accrued interest
- how the securities should be delivered for the sale and redelivered for the repurchase
- where payments should be made (the banking details of each party)
- arrangements for the provision of additional margin in the event of a fall in the market value of securities held as collateral.

Interest accrues on securities over time, and it is important to establish which party is entitled to interest accruing during the loan period, between the original sale and the repurchase. Similarly, it is important to establish who is entitled to receive any interest payments made on securities during the time they are held as collateral in a repo. For example, a bank may hold $10 million of 6% US Treasury bonds as collateral in a repo, and during the term of the repo interest of $300,000 may be paid on these bonds. Would the bank be entitled to keep the interest as purchaser of the bonds?

In a standard repo agreement, entitlement to all accrued interest during the term of the repo, and entitlement to all interest payments, if any, during the term of the repo, belongs to the party selling the securities and making the subsequent repurchase.

Once a Master Agreement has been arranged between two parties, each individual repo transaction is agreed by telephone or by electronic message. The individual transactions will contain data specific to the transaction, such as:

- acknowledgment that the transaction forms part of and is subject to the terms and conditions of the global master agreement
- the contract date
- details of the purchased securities, and their identifying number or numbers, e.g. their ISIN numbers
- the margin percentage
- the sale value of the securities
- the sale date and the repurchase date
- the contractual currency
- the repo rate (interest rate)
- the basis for calculating interest, e.g. actual/360-day basis.

Securities Traded as Collateral

Repo agreements in theory can involve any security, but in practise the majority of transactions involve high credit quality securities such as government stocks and securities issued by highly rated companies. The most active repo market is in US Treasury notes and bonds.

The maturity of the securities must be longer than the term of the repo. For example, if the term of a repo transaction is two weeks, securities provided as collateral must not include any securities maturing during that two-week period.

Because repos essentially are short-term secured loans, the securities that are sold and repurchased are referred to as collateral, i.e. security for a loan. The collateral that is asked for might be specific, with the customer asking to buy and resell a specific bond. Collateral also might be general, with the customer willing to accept any bonds meeting credit quality and value requirements.

Special Features of Repo Agreements	
Purpose:	To make secured loans.
Term:	Short-term, overnight or longer. Possibly open-ended.
Ownership of securities:	Title passes to the buyer at the time of the sale.
Ownership of income from securities:	If interest is paid by the issuer of securities during the repo term, the buyer will receive the payment, but undertakes to remit this to the seller.
Collateral margin:	The borrower will maintain collateral to a percentage amount in excess of the loan amount.
Marking to market:	The collateral is revalued to current market value each day. If the collateral falls in value below a certain amount, e.g. below the amount lent, the borrower can call for additional securities as collateral.

Special Features of Repo Agreements (continued)	
Marking to market (cont.):	Conversely, if the collateral rises in value above a certain amount, the borrower can call for the excess collateral to be returned by the lender.
Substitution (if granted):	Although the borrower has sold securities for the term of the repo, he can call them back at any time, so long as he substitutes other securities of equal market value. Substitution can be made any number of times during the term of a repo.
Netting:	Payments between the parties relating to different individual repo transactions can be netted, with just one payment by one party to the other for all the repo transactions settled between the parties on any given day.
Redelivery at the repurchase date:	The lender has to sell back equivalent securities. For example, if bonds in paper form are provided as collateral, the borrower must deliver equivalent bonds at the repurchase date that may be bond certificates from the same issue, but with different serial numbers.

Settlement

Arrangements for the transfer of cash and collateral at the start and end of a repo period must ensure that the seller of the securities receives payment from the buyer and at the same time the buyer receives securities in return. The settlement arrangements must be secure otherwise there would be significant credit risk or counterparty risk in repo transactions.

- When the securities are in paper form, they probably will be immobilized and held by an organization providing a safekeeping service. Both parties to the repo transaction will have accounts with the major central securities depositories, such as the DTCC in the US, and Clearstream and Euroclear in Europe and Crest in the UK. The sale of securities will be transacted by book entry, with a transfer of the securities from the account of the seller (borrower) to the account of the buyer (lender). Payment will be made through the assured payments system of the central securities depository. At the repurchase date similar transactions will occur, but in the reverse direction.

- When the securities are issued in dematerialized form, and exist only within the book-entry system of a central securities depository, transfers and payments are by delivery versus payment within the system.

Payment and physical delivery might both take some time to arrange, and settlement of the initial sale to take place one or two days after the date of the repo transaction agreement. Instructions to settle a transaction may, for example, be given through the Clearstream or Euroclear clearing systems. If the customer gives payment instructions two business days prior to settlement, and if the transaction is agreed on Monday, the settlement (delivery versus payment) will take place on Wednesday.

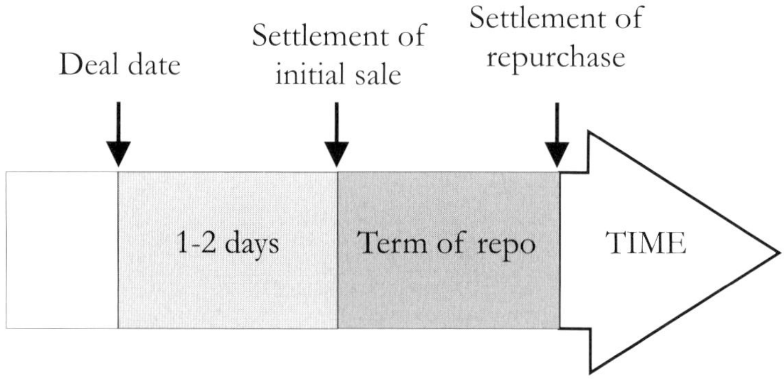

However, with improvements in the systems of central securities depositories, settlement on the same date as the transaction is made has become a possibility.

At maturity, the securities will be sold back by the borrower to the lender at a price that includes interest for the term between the sale and repurchase.

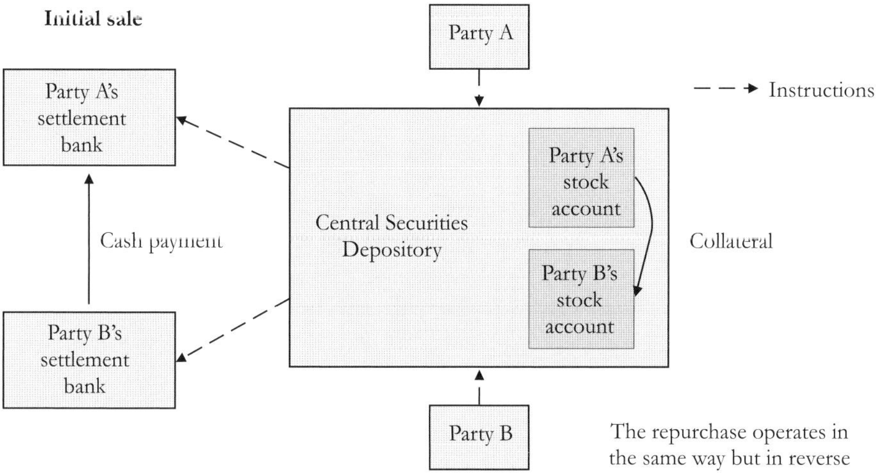

Repo Transaction Mathematics

The borrower and lender will agree on the size of the transaction. The borrower might require a specific amount of funds for a given term, or the lender might have a specific amount of funds to lend. Once the size of the loan has been established, the parties will then agree the nature and current market value of the securities to be provided as collateral.

The quantity of securities provided will depend on their value and on the size of the transaction. Their value is their current market value, plus accrued interest, with a possible downwards adjustment to give comfort to the lender that the securities should offer adequate collateral.

Example 1
Able Bank makes a seven-day repo agreement with Baker for

$50 million. Collateral will be provided by 8% US Treasury bonds that have a market value of 102.00. It is agreed that their value for the purpose of the repo should be 101.00, and that the interest rate payable should be 7.5% per annum.

Analysis
The repo transaction will involve the purchase and resale of bonds with a nominal value of $49,504,950 ($50 million ÷ 101 × 100). Able Bank will in effect borrow $50 million and provide bonds with a face value of $49,504,950 as collateral. At maturity of the repo agreement, Able Bank will pay Baker $50 million plus interest at 7.5% per annum, and Baker will return the securities.

The current market value of the Treasuries provided as collateral, at 102.00, is $50,495,049. The size of the margin therefore is $495,049.

The repo interest is:

$$\$50 \text{ million} \times 7.5\% \times 7/360 = \$72,917$$

At the repurchase date, Able Bank will pay Baker the $50 million borrowed plus the interest, $50,072,917 in total.

The repurchase price of the bonds therefore is:

$$\frac{\$50,072,917}{\$49,504,950} \times 100 = 101.147$$

Example 2
An investment company has $100 million to invest on a Monday and enters into a seven-day repo agreement with a bank. The securities are 4% US Treasury bonds that have a market price of 96.0. No margin is requested. However, the market value of the bonds for the purpose of establishing the quantity of collateral required will include accrued interest. Accrued interest on these bonds is 1.1 points. The repo dealer's offer rate is 6.5%. The transaction will be on a delivery-versus-payment (DVP) basis.

Analysis

The initial sale of 4% US Treasury bonds is by the bank to the investment company.

If two days are needed for settlement the initial sale will be settled on Wednesday, and for a seven-day repo, the repurchase will be settled on the Wednesday following.

Because the company wishes to lend $100 million, and there is no margin or haircut requirement, the nominal value of the bonds that are provided as collateral will be:

$$P \times \frac{100}{(MV + A)}$$

Where:

P is the amount of the money to be lent by the investor
MV is the market value of the securities
A is the accrued interest on the securities (in points).

In this example, the T-bonds provided as collateral should be bonds with a nominal value of:

$$\$100 \text{ million} \times \frac{100}{(96.0 + 1.1)} = \$102{,}986{,}612$$

The repurchase price will be the original sale price plus interest at the repo rate of 6.5% per annum. Interest will be:

$$6.5\% \times 7/360 \times \$100 \text{ million} = \$126{,}389.$$

The repurchase price therefore will be $100,126,389. This represents a price for the bonds of:

$$\frac{\$100{,}126{,}389}{\$102{,}986{,}612} \times 100 = 97.22$$

Repo

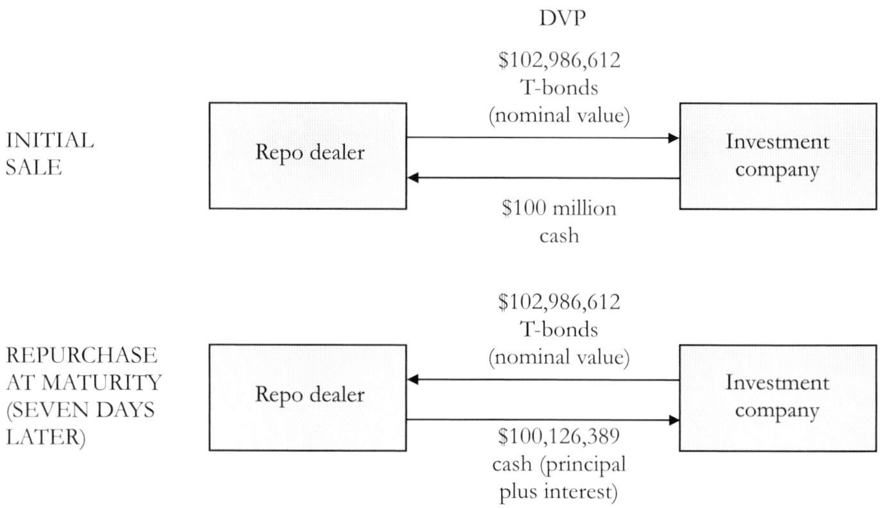

The investment company in effect has invested $100 million for seven days against collateral of about $103 million (nominal value) of US government Treasury bonds, and earned interest at 6.5% per annum.

Reverse Repo

A reverse repo is a repurchase agreement in which a dealer buys securities from a customer and at the same time promises to sell them back at a future date at an agreed price. Whereas a repo is a form of money-market lending, a reverse repo is a form of money-market investment.

Reverse Agreement

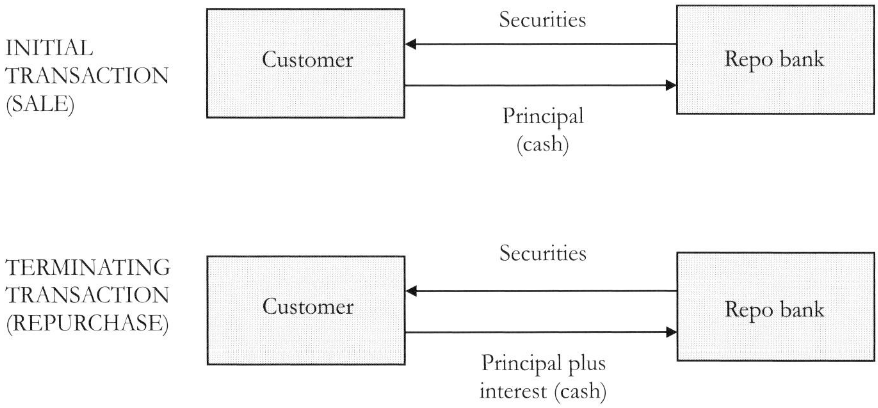

Although repo and reverse repo transactions have been defined from the viewpoint of a repo dealer, it may be apparent that in any repo transaction, one party is making a repo transaction, selling securities for subsequent repurchase, and the other party is making a reverse transaction. A repo and a reverse repo are simply opposite sides of the same transaction.

Repo Rates

Repo dealers, banks specializing in repo transactions, will quote two repo prices, for repos of a given term – overnight, one week, two weeks, etc.

- The bid price is the price that the dealer is willing to accept in return for purchasing bonds and agreeing to sell them back. The bid rate therefore is the repo rate for a customer. The customer's repo is the dealer's reverse repo.
- The offer rate is the rate that the dealer is willing to pay to sell and repurchase bonds. The offer rate therefore is the rate at which a customer can transact a reverse repo. The customer's reverse is the dealer's repo.

The bid rate is higher than the offer rate. Bid-offer spreads on dollar repos typically are five to ten basis points (0.05% - 0.10%).

Example
An investment company contacts a bank that makes a market in repos and asks for the bank's rates on seven-day repos in euros. The bank gives rates of 3.50-3.45%. The investment company then asks for a seven-day repo agreement and buys German government securities from the repo bank to a value of €100 million.

The securities that will be used as collateral are 6% Bunds that have a market value of 102.5. Accumulated interest is 1.0.

Analysis
The nominal value of the Bunds to be delivered is
€100 million × 100/(102.5 + 1.0) = €96,618,357. These will be delivered in exchange for a payment of €100 million by the investment company.

The repo rate is 3.45% per annum. At the maturity of the repo, the Bunds will be delivered back to the repo bank in exchange for a payment of €100 million plus interest. Interest will be
€100 × 3.45% × 7/360 = €67,083.33.

The repurchase price will be €100,067,083.33.

Why Are Repos Used?

The private repo market, as distinct from the repo market used by governments for their open-market operations, grew out of the need of financial markets professionals to carry their inventories of securities in the most cost-effective manner. Market dealers use their securities to raise temporary cash, and achieve lower interest costs on the borrowing because of the quality of the bonds and bills provided as collateral.

Repos offer investors attractive yields on short-term investments, combined with top-quality collateral. When an investor deposits funds with a bank, it relies only on the good credit of the bank. In contrast, an investment in repos provides two layers of protection:

- the credit risk of the repo counterparty, and
- the collateral of a government bond that is risk-free, or of other securities with a high credit rating, usually AA or AAA rated.

Repo also has grown as a market for interbank borrowing, where the lender is prepared to accept a lower interest rate than on interbank loans, in return for the benefit of the lending being collateralized.

Benefits of Repos

Lender	Borrower
A favorable balance between risk and return	Low cost of carry
High-quality collateral that is marked-to-market daily to maintain coverage	Excess collateral can be recalled
Open repos have features similar to an on-call deposit	Positions can be rolled forward one day at a time
Can access specific collateral, i.e. particular types or issues of securities	Collateral can be substituted during the term of a transaction

Matched Book Trading in Repos and Reverses

At some banks, repos have developed from an instrument for short-term lower-cost borrowing into a traded product for making profits. The private repo market is driven by these market-making banks.

Market makers in repos run matched books, using repos to borrow at one rate and reverse repos to lend at a higher rate, taking the spread between the lending and the borrowing rates as profit.

They also may use repos to trade in short-term interest-rate risk, by mismatching the maturities of repos (borrowing cash) and reverses (lending cash). For example borrowing through one-week repos and lending through two-week reverse repos creates a mismatch, with exposure to changes in the two-week rate of interest in one week's time. A repo dealer will assess the risks involved in taking this position, and will take it on if, in his/her view, repo rates are unlikely to change to the extent that money will be lost on the mismatch. In making such trades, the repo dealer may decide to use interest-rate-futures contracts to manage the risk.

Essentially this is the same kind of risk-taking as carried out by money-market traders in a commercial bank; the difference is that in matched book trading the risk-takers are securities-markets professionals, using collateralized loans as their instruments.

Example: Creating a Tail with Repo

Suppose the yield curve currently is strongly positive and interest rates are higher for loans and money-market instruments with longer maturities. Delta Bank's trader does not foresee a change either in the shape of the yield curve or in the general level of interest rates. Three-month LIBOR is 5.50% and one-year LIBOR is 6.0%. Delta Bank can invest in government securities for one year at 6.0% for example, and repo the securities to another investor for three months at 5.60%, that is a 10-basis point (0.10%) premium on three-month LIBOR.

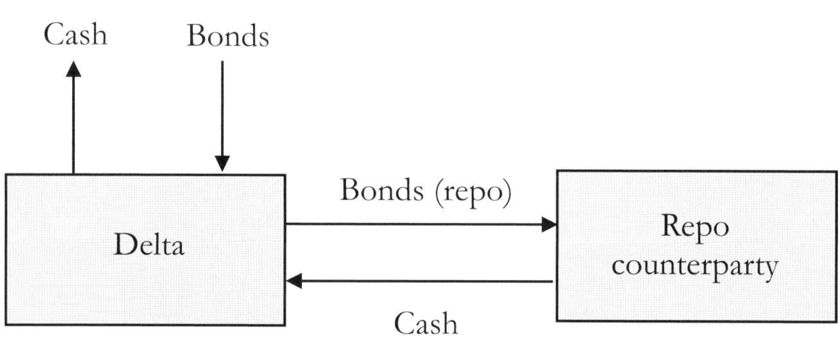

Analysis

The repo finances Delta's bond purchase. For the first three months of the transaction the bank earns a profit of 40 basis points because it earns interest at 6% on the securities but pays interest of just 5.60% on the repo.

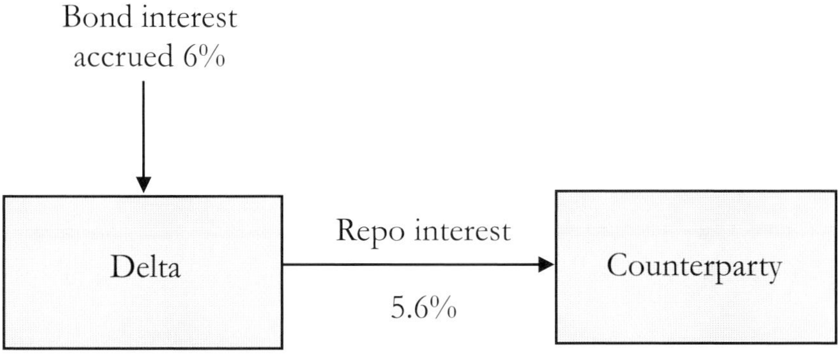

At the end of three months the bank can, if it wishes, use the same securities in further repo agreements, expecting to continue to profit on the interest-rate differentials. The risk for Delta Bank is that the level of short-term interest rates will rise and for the remaining nine-month term of the security the bank will have to offer yields closer to or even higher than 6.0% to place the bonds in the repo market.

For example when the first repo matures, three-month LIBOR might have risen to 6.0% and the rate for a three-month repo to 6.20%. If Delta Bank arranged another three-month repo using the securities as collateral, the value of the securities would be lower because interest rates have gone up, and the cost of borrowing through repos also has gone up to the point where the bank is making a loss of 20 basis points (6.20% - 6.00%).

Banks also might identify particular securities that are well suited for use as collateral in repo agreements, such as floating-rate securities with a long maturity issued by a quality institution.

Sell/Buyback Transactions

A buy/sell transaction, known in the US as a dollar roll, is a form of repo transaction in which a customer buys the securities from the repo dealer and simultaneously agrees a separate sell-back transaction for the securities for a future date. There are two transactions rather than just one repo transaction.

The main difference between a straight repo and a buy/sell transaction concerns the rights to the interest on the securities over the term from the sale to repurchase. In a straight repo, it is the original seller and repurchaser who retains the right to the interest. In a buy/sell transaction, in contrast, accrued interest belongs to the customer who buys and resells the securities.

The important point to note is that in a sell/buyback transaction, the temporary purchaser is entitled to accrued interest on the securities. Accordingly, the repurchase price has to be adjusted.

Example: sell/buyback transaction
A dealer sells and buys back €1 million of 4.5% German government bonds for seven days. The terms of the sell/buyback are:

Bond	4.5% bond, maturing February 20, 2015
Nominal value	€1 million
Sale date	November 23 (273 days accrued interest)
Buyback date	November 30 (280 days accrued interest)
Sale price	100.28
Repo rate	5.0625%

Analysis
Initial sale
Clean price of bonds sold:

$$€1{,}000{,}000 \times \frac{100.28}{100.00} = €1{,}002{,}800.00$$

Accrued interest on these bonds at time of sale:

$$€1,000,000 \times \frac{273}{360} \times 4.5\% = €34,125.00$$

Settlement amount for the sale:

€1,002,800.00 + 34,125.00 – 1,036,925.00.

Repurchase

		€
Interest accrued during the repo period	€1,000,000 × 4.50% × 7/360	875.00
Repo interest	€1,036,925.00 × 5.0625% × 7/360	1,020.72
Difference		- 145.72

This difference should be expressed as a percentage of the nominal value of the bonds. This is (– 145.72/1,000,000) × 100% = 0.014572.

The repurchase price for the bonds therefore should be:
100.28 – 0.014572 = 100.265428.

The actual cash flow on the repurchase date is the forward sale price times €1 million (nominal value), plus the total accrued interest on the bonds up to the buyback settlement date. In this example, the accrued interest is for 280 days.

		€
Forward repurchase price	€1,000,000 × 100.265428/100.00	1,002,654.28
Accrued interest	€1,000,000 × 4.50% × 280/360	35,000.00
Difference		1,037,654.28

Looked at from the point of view of the buyer/subsequent seller (borrower), the transaction gives the following return:

	€
Money lent	- 1,036,925.00
Money repaid on buyback	+ 1,037,654.28
Gain	+ 729.28

This represents a yield, on an annualized basis, of (729.28/1,036,925.00) × (360/7) × 100% = 3.0625%, that is the repo rate.

Overnight, Term and Open Repos

Repos also can be described by their maturity. An overnight repo, common in the US, involves an initial sale on one day and a repurchase on the following day. A term repo is for a specified maturity. Repos normally have a specified term to maturity, but in an open transaction the dealer and customer/lender agree that the money should be provided for an unspecified term, with either party able to terminate the agreement at any time. For open repos, the interest rate can change from day to day, depending on changes in market conditions.

Repos are an over-the-counter product, and there is no dealers' association. Market statistics therefore are unavailable, but the size of the market appears to have grown rapidly and is now very large.

The dollar repo market in the US has developed sufficiently for standardized documentation to be available. The market has low-cost clearance using the Fedwire service, and a screen-based pricing information system.

The main repo market is in dollars, but the Canadian dollar market, although much smaller, is now well developed. Other developing repo markets are in Deutschemarks, French francs and the Ecu. In Europe, settlement is through Euroclear or Cedel, or possibly in the country of origin of the securities, with settlement usually on a two-day basis. In Canada, clearance is via Euroclear or CDS. There is also a developing repo market in the yen.

The repo market has developed as a short-term lending market because of the difficulties of many banks, particularly in the US, in borrowing or attracting deposits at satisfactory rates of interest for the bank. Borrowing rates can be reduced by offering top-quality collateral in the form of third-party market securities such as government bonds.

As with other money-market instruments, repos offer an alternative method of investment with a different balance of return, risk and maturities.

8

Back-Office Operations

The front office in an institution dealing in the financial markets is the dealing office where transactions are made by the dealers. Once a transaction has been executed, it has to be settled. Back-office operations of an organization are concerned with matters such as:

- administration of the organization's money-market investments
- settlement of purchases or sales of MMIs.

MMIs: Paper or Electronic Form?

Traditionally, money-market instruments such as bills, CDs and CP, have been issued in paper form, printed on special security paper. However, money-market instruments are bearer instruments, and there is a serious risk to owners of physical loss of the bill or certificate. Investment institutions place their paper instruments with a bank or other institution providing custody services, to safeguard their investments.

When bearer instruments are sold, and the instruments are in paper form, they have to be transferred from the seller to the buyer, or from the seller's custodian to the buyer's custodian. There are risks and costs associated with physical transfers of bearer instruments.

A more secure arrangement, avoiding the need for paper certificates to be physically moved, is for the same organization to act as safekeeper for all the paper instruments. If one organization holds everything, the instruments can be immobilized, and there is no need to move them when they are sold by one investor to another. The transfer of ownership can be recorded in a computer system in which investors each have an account for recording their ownership of investments.

Because paper instruments may be immobilized at a central depository, and ownership recorded by computer, the need for paper instruments can be questioned. Instruments could be issued in electronic form, without any underlying piece of paper. This would save the expense of printing the instruments as well as the costs of storage and custody. However, for instruments to be issued in electronic form, it must be possible by law for a computer record to represent the legal ownership of a financial instrument.

When financial instruments are fully dematerialized, the computer records of ownership must be retained either within the same computer system, or within two or more computer systems that are able to communicate with each other, and make transfers of ownership between them. An organization that operates a book-entry system of ownership of financial instruments is known as a central securities depository.

When ownership of financial instruments is represented by computer records in a book-entry system, transfers of ownership following a secondary market sale are recorded within the system. In addition, however, there have to be arrangements for:

- new issues of instruments, and
- payment by the issuer. In the case of money-market instruments, the issuer of bills, CDs or CP must make a payment at maturity of the instrument.

Traditionally, when money-market instruments were issued in paper form, the bill or certificate was given to the investor. To receive payment at maturity, the holder of the instrument would present the bill or certificate for payment at a designated payment bank.

When money-market instruments are issued in paper form and immobilized at a central depository, payments at maturity can be made to the depository that can arrange for the money to be paid to the owners of the instruments.

When money-market instruments are issued in dematerialized form, they are created by entering a new issue of instruments in the computer system, and at maturity, full payment is made by the issuer to the investors through the central system.

Dematerialization of MMIs: the UK Experience

The UK provides an interesting example of money markets switching from being primarily a market for paper instruments to a market for dematerialized instruments. The changeover is expected to occur during 2001 or 2002.

Prior to a project to dematerialize most money-market instruments, MMIs in the UK have been:

- in paper form
- bearer instruments, and tradable (negotiable) in a secondary market
- not fungible
- not settled in an assured payments system.

Instruments are fungible when they are grouped in the same class, and all instruments in the same class have identical characteristics. When fungible instruments are bought and sold, it does not matter which particular instruments within the class are exchanged. When instruments are not fungible, each has unique characteristics, and each is a separate instrument. For this reason, they are bought and sold individually.

An assured payments system is one in which transactions are settled by delivery versus payment or DVP. The issuer or seller delivers the instruments to the buyer, and is guaranteed simultaneous payment in return.

Prior to the introduction of the new system, most Treasury bills and a large quantity of bank bills, commercial bills, CDs and CP were held in immobilized form within a central depository called the Central

Moneymarkets Office (CMO), ownership of which was transferred to Crest in 1999.

The UK is in the process of changing to a system for the wholesale market in money-market instruments where:

- money-market instruments are issued in dematerialized form, without paper bills or certificates, within the Crest central securities depository system
- they are negotiable
- they are fungible, and even can be traded in flexible amounts, with traded amounts denominated in units of one penny
- they are settled by an assured-payments system, with payment in central bank funds within the Crest system.

The new system will be capable of settlement of repo transactions, as well as transactions involving straightforward purchases of instruments in Treasury bills, bills of exchange, CDs and CP.

Some paper money-market instruments may continue to be issued for certain types of transaction, and for the benefit of retail investors.

Issues of MMIs

As part of the requirements for dematerialization of MMIs, it is important to create fungibility. Traditionally, many bills of exchange and CDs have been for specific transactions and issued individually. Some instruments have been more fungible: for example, all the 91-day Treasury bills issued on a particular date have exactly the same features and so can be traded as a single issue. Similarly, with an issue of commercial paper on the same date and for the same maturity, the features of all the issued paper is the same, and therefore it can be traded as an issue.

For money-market instruments to be fungible, and treated as part of a single issue, they must:

- be issued/accepted by the same organization
- have the same maturity date, and

- in the case of interest-bearing instruments, have the same coupon or rate of interest on nominal value.

An issue of dematerialized MMIs will be created within the Crest system, with a unique identification code (ISIN number). Holdings of investments within the same issue are interchangable, and can be divided into smaller holdings if required.

New issues will be entered into the Crest system, and the record of ownership within Crest will represent legal title to the instruments. There will be no requirement for paper instruments.

When MMIs are purchased, payment will be made through the Crest assured-payments system. The settlement banks used by investors will be required to make payment in their central bank funds at the Bank of England.

Summary

The characteristics of the money markets continue to undergo major changes, with clearing and settlement systems switching from traditional paper settlement without DVP to electronic settlement and assured payments with DVP. The experience of the London markets in switching wholesale operations to a dematerialized system is particularly interesting, given the size and significance of London as a money-market center.

9

Open-Market Operations

Open-market operations refers to the operations of the government or a government agency in the money markets. Central governments are active on a daily basis in the money markets for three main reasons.

- The government raises short-term funds in the money markets by issuing bills on a regular basis. In the US and the UK for example, there is a weekly issue of bills for which institutions are invited to make an offer/put in a bid.
- Due to payments between the banking system and the central government, there may be an overall shortage of funds within the commercial banking system. The government will seek to provide funds to the banking system through the money markets so that there is adequate funding of the banking system each day. This helps to achieve a reasonable stability in interest rates.
- The government also can use its operations in the markets to influence or control the level of short-term interest rates. This is a major aspect of economic policy in advanced economies, including the US, UK and the countries of the euro zone.

There are three ways in which the government or its agency carries out its open-market operations:

- by purchasing or selling money-market instruments
- by making transactions in repo
- by short-term lending direct to banks with a shortage of funds.

Money in the Banking System

To appreciate how open-market operations work, it is necessary to have a broad understanding of how money flows between banks and the government.

All large commercial banks have an account with the central bank of their country. In the US, commercial banks have an account with their district Federal Reserve Bank. In the UK, the commercial banks have an account with the Bank of England. Money in the banking system can be represented mainly by the deposits of bank customers. The central government, however, maintains its own account with the central bank, and does not use the commercial banks.

Rules vary between countries, but the government may have regulations requiring the banks to maintain a minimum amount of funds in their account with the central bank. This minimum may be called minimum reserve requirements. The minimum reserves a bank has to keep will be recalculated regularly, and based on the size of the bank and its liabilities.

Funds held by commercial banks with the central bank earn little or no interest. In the euro zone of EU countries, the Eurosystem countries, banks are paid interest on their minimum reserve deposits with their national central bank, but no interest at all on any balances in excess of the minimum.

On each banking day, the commercial banks settle payments between their customers. If a customer of Bank X makes a payment to a customer of Bank Y, the payment is settled by a transfer of funds from Bank X to Bank Y. On any day, banks will be required to make a net payment to some banks, and will receive net payments from others. The payments are settled by means of a transfer of funds across the accounts with the central bank.

As a result of these payments, some banks will have funds with the central bank in excess of what they need or are required to maintain there. Other banks, on the other hand, may face a shortage of funds.

- Banks forecasting a surplus of funds at the central bank on a given day will take measures to use the surplus to earn a return. They will invest in money-market instruments, buying bills, CDs and CP, or will put the money on deposit with other financial institutions, or will lend the money to other banks in the interbank market.
- Banks forecasting that they will have insufficient funds at the central bank that day will take measures to overcome the shortage. They may do this by selling money-market investments, or by withdrawing money on deposit at call with other institutions, or by borrowing on the interbank market. They also might deal with the government or its agency, in open-market transactions.

Provided that the banking system as a whole has sufficient funds on a given day, the funds will be redistributed through interbank dealing and other money-market transactions.

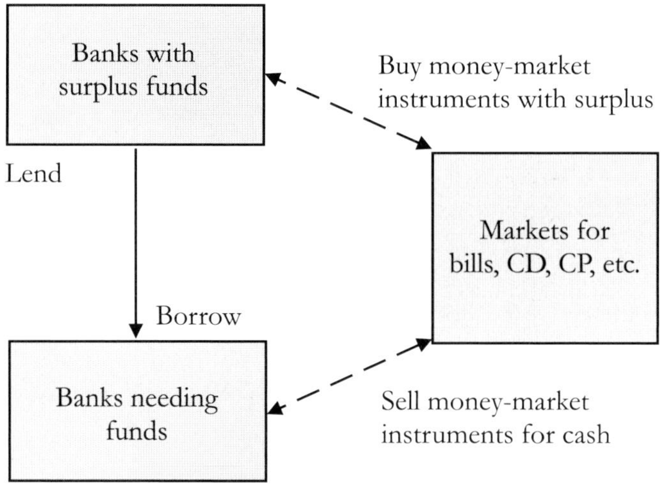

The Government and Money in the Banking System
The total amount of funds in the banking system, and therefore the liquidity of the system, is strongly affected by the government.

Money paid by the banks or by customers of the banks, is transferred from the banks' accounts with the central bank to the government's account. As a result, the money leaves the banking system. On the other hand, when the government makes payments to the banks or to customers of the banks, there is a flow of money into the banking system.

Money therefore will be withdrawn from the banking system when the government issues bills, notes or bonds. These have to be paid for. Banks and other investors acquire the securities, but give money to the government in return. Money will be put back into the banking system when the government buys bills and other money-market instruments from the market, or when it redeems issues of debt.

The central government also takes money out of the banking system when it collects taxes, but puts money back into the system when it spends.

Transfers of funds between the banks and the central government therefore can create either an overall surplus of funds in the banking system, or an overall shortage.

When a government uses open-market operations to control interest rates, it ensures that the banking system usually has a shortage of funds on any particular day. This will force the banks to obtain short-term money from the central government. Because the government is supplying much-needed short-term funds, it is able to exert a very strong influence over the level of interest rates in the money market. Control, or very strong influence, over short-term rates has a knock-on effect into the banking market as a whole, and affects important commercial interest rates, such as bank lending rates and home-loan rates.

Matching Supply and Demand for Money in the Banking System

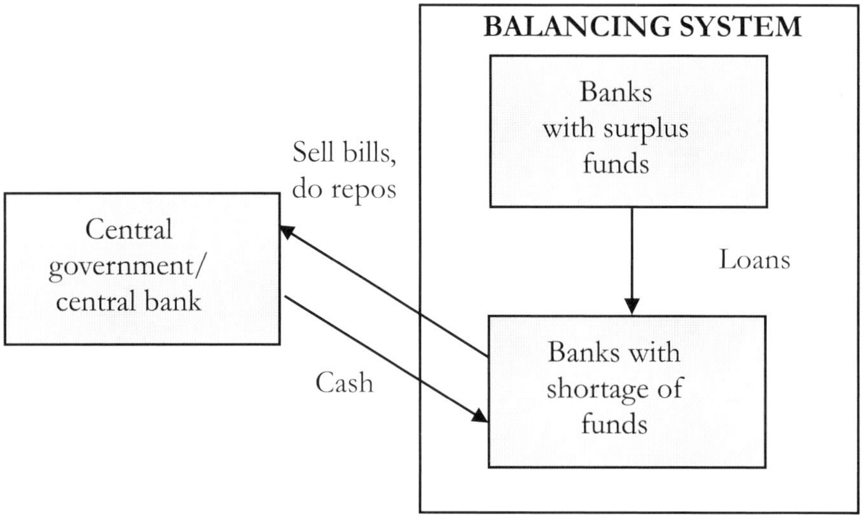

Open-Market Operations: the Transactions

Open-market operations are carried out by an agent of the central government. In the US, this is the open-market desk of the New York Federal District Bank. In the UK, the responsibility is shared between the Debt Management Office and the Bank of England. In the Eurosystem, the European Central Bank determines interest-rate policy, but operations are conducted by each of the national central banks within the system.

The transactions used in open-market operations are:

- repos or reverse repos
- buying or selling bills and eligible money-market instruments
- occasionally, direct short-term lending, sometimes referred to as discount window lending.

Open-market operations are conducted only with approved or eligible institutions with which the government agency will deal.

When the government wants to alleviate a shortage of money in the banking system, it can provide the money by entering into reverse repo transactions with eligible institutions (banks). To the institution, the transaction is a repo.

- In the first leg of the repo, the bank sells securities to the government and receives cash in return. The securities must be on a list of securities acceptable to the government as collateral for a repo transaction.
- In the second leg, the bank buys back the securities, and makes a money payment in return.

As with any other repo transaction, the bank uses the repo to borrow short-term. The government agency is able to determine the rate of interest at which the repos are transacted, and through its influence on the repo rate, will influence interest rates in the rest of the banking system.

An alternative to repos is the outright purchase of government bills and other money market instruments, such as bank bills. The government provides money to the sellers of the instruments. If it purchase sit own bills, the purchase cancels its obligation to pay at maturity. If it purchases other instruments, it will be entitled to the payment at maturity. In purchasing money market instruments, the government will only agree to purchase instruments that it considers eligible. Bank bills that the government would be prepared to purchase in open market operations are known as eligible bank bills, and these command finer rates of discount in the market than bank bills that are not eligible for sale to the government.

The discount rate or yield at which the government will buy bills in its open market operations helps to influence interest rates in the rest of the banking system.

Open-Market Operations in the UK

Open-market operations by the Bank of England are used both to provide liquidity to the banking system, and also to allow the Monetary Policy Committee of the Bank to control interest rates in the UK money markets, through its decisions about the repo rate and the rate of discount for its outright purchases of bills.

In its open-market operations, the Bank of England uses both repo transactions, sale to the Bank and subsequent repurchase of eligible securities and instruments, and the outright purchase of eligible bills.

In its repo transactions, the Bank will accept as collateral, i.e. will buy, any of the following:

- UK government bonds and notes (gilts, including gilt strips)
- sterling Treasury bills
- Bank of England euro bills
- eligible bank bills
- eligible local authority bills
- marketable debt of the UK government in currencies other than sterling
- securities denominated in sterling and issued by governments of the European Economic Area (EEA) or an approved international institution
- securities denominated in euros and issued by governments or central banks of the European Economic Area (EEA) or an approved international institution.

The Bank of England participates in various central security depository systems, such as those of Clearstream and Euroclear, in order to accept these securities as collateral. Securities offered as collateral must have a remaining maturity longer than the term of the repo, so that they do not reach maturity during the term of the repo.

The Bank also will offer to purchase, in an outright sale:

- sterling Treasury bills
- eligible bank bills with an original maturity of no more than 187 days
- eligible local authority bills.

Daily Open-Market Operation Procedures of the Bank of England

The Bank will publish a forecast of the liquidity position of the banking system at around 9.45 a.m. each day, and will invite offers for repos and for the outright purchase of bills. The screen announcement will take the following form.

> 9.45 am. Initial liquidity forecast. Stg 160 mn shortage. A round of fixed-rate operations is invited. The Bank's repo rate is 4.75%. The operations will comprise repos to 5 March, 6 March and 7 March and outright offers of bills maturing on or before 6 March.
>
> Principal factors in the forecast …

The Bank normally will invite repos to any or all of three maturity dates, a date two weeks forward, and the working days on either side of this date. The rate at which the Bank will deal is usually fixed, and announced on the screen. Occasionally, the Bank may invite tenders.

Tenders must be submitted promptly, and the Bank will make its allotments within 15 minutes of inviting offers in any round of its open-market operations.

During the morning and early afternoon, the liquidity forecast for the banking system for the day is revised, and a new screen message sent out at 2.30 p.m., with a further round of open-market operations invited. The screen message might be as follows:

> 2.30 pm. Liquidity forecast revision. Stg 170 mn shortage. Residual shortage – Stg 45 mn. A round of fixed-rate operations is invited.
>
> The Bank's repo rate is 4.75%. The operations will comprise repos to 5 March, 6 March and 7 March and outright offers of bills maturing on or before 6 March.

The two main rounds of open-market operations are at 9.45 a.m. and 2.30 p.m. each day, and at about 2.45 the Bank will announce the results of these two rounds, stating the amount of funds allotted, divided into funds allotted through repos and funds allotted through outright purchases of bills.

> 2.45 pm. Total amount allotted – Stg 170 mn of which outright - Stg 25 mn, repo – Stg 145 mn.

Each month, the Monetary Policy Committee of the Bank of England, the body responsible for interest-rate policy in the UK, meets to decide what the level of interest rates should be. On the days it makes its announcement, the decision is published around noon by the Bank, and the first round of open-market operations is delayed until 12.15.

Occasionally, when the first two rounds of open-market operations appear to have been insufficient to mop up the shortage of funds in the banking system, the bank will invite a third round of open-market operations at 3.30 p.m., to mop up the residual shortage. All transactions in this third round would be overnight repos. To discourage late dealing by banks in this third round, the repo rate applied to these transactions normally will be at 100 basis points (1%) above the Bank's prevailing repo rate.

Occasionally there may be a fourth round of open-market operations at 4.20 p.m., where there is still a residual shortage of funds in the market. This round of operations would consist of repo transactions.

Repo Transactions

The Bank's repo transactions conform to normal repos in the market, with the difference that the Bank's ground rules for dealing are well-publicized.

- The Bank specifies the type of security it will accept as collateral.
- It requires securities as collateral to the value of the repurchase

price, and the Bank has specified its rules for establishing the market value of each type of security, and the size of the margin or haircut it will take off this market value.

Example

The Bank has outstanding repo transactions with a participant in the market, Epsilon Bank, in which the total repurchase price for the securities held by the Bank (the collateral) is £325,257,000.

The Bank will monitor continually the current market value of the securities it holds as collateral from Epsilon Bank. Suppose that it makes the following calculation

Securities	**Market value**	**Appropriate margin ratio**	**Adjusted market value**
	£ million		**£ million**
Gilts with a remaining maturity of 3-7 years	112.450	1.015	110.788
Gilts with a remaining maturity of over 7 years	99.400	1.025	96.976
Euro-denominated securities issued by EEA central governments with remaining maturity of 1-3 years	49.800	1.030	48.350
Sterling bills	67.350	1.0025	67.182
Total	329.000		323.296
Repurchase amount			325.257
Margin deficit			1.961

In this example, there is a margin deficit of nearly £2 million. The Bank will call for extra securities as margin from Epsilon Bank if the deficit exceeds a call trigger amount, an amount the Bank decides at its own discretion. If the Bank were to make an additional margin call on Epsilon Bank in this example, the adjusted market value of the additional securities supplied would have to be equal to at least the margin deficit of £1.961 million.

Gilt Repo Rates
Gilt repo transactions are repo transactions where UK government securities are provided as the collateral. Gilt repo rates therefore should, in principle, be close to risk-free interest rates for sterling.

Operations of the Debt Management Office
Whereas the Bank of England is responsible for monetary policy and control over interest rates and the rate of inflation, the Debt Management Office is responsible for issuing bills and bonds on behalf of the government, and to ensure that the banking system is not adversely affected by cash flows between the banks and the government. The DMO works closely with the Bank of England, and as part of its operations, it may:

- make a new issue of government bonds under a *standing repo facility*, and
- cancel the bonds on their eventual repurchase.

A typical announcement by the DMO to the market might be as follows:

> An additional £574 million of 5 ¾% Treasury Stock 2009 has today been created and made available to the market under the DMO's standing repo facility, introduced on 1 June 2000. It is intended that this additional stock will be canceled on return. The DMO has been given general collateral at the Bank of England's repo rate against the stock it has lent.

Open-Market Operations in the Eurosystem

The European Central Bank conducts its operations in the money markets through the national central banks of countries in the euro zone. Collectively the ECB and the national central banks make up what is called the Eurosystem.

Eligible institutions are banks and other institutions that are permitted to deal in the open-market operations of the central banks. Each eligible institution must maintain a minimum level of reserves with its central bank. The minimum reserve system is designed to ensure that there is a structural shortage of liquidity in the banking system. The minimum balance that each eligible institution must maintain with its central bank is an amount equal to 2% of its average eligible liabilities over a maintenance period, usually one month.

The main types of transaction used are reverse repos. There are two types.

- The Main Refinancing Operation (MRO) is conducted weekly, and the repos have a maturity of two weeks. The MRO provides the bulk of the liquidity required by the banking system. It is conducted by means of fixed-rate tenders, with the ECB stating the rate it requires, and institutions being invited to tender for business at that rate. The MRO therefore is used by the ECB to signal its main refinancing rate.
- The Long-Term Refinancing Operation (LTRO) is conducted monthly, and the repos have a three-month maturity. The ECB does not state a fixed rate of interest for these transactions, and institutions are invited to put in auction bids. The highest bids are accepted. Originally, the auction was conducted on Dutch-auction rules, all repos being transacted at the same rate that was the minimum accepted rate from the bids received. They are now conducted on American-auction rules, successful bidders pay the rate they bid, so that transactions are made at differing rates. The LTRO is not used by the ECB as a signalling mechanism for interest rates.

Controlling Interest Rates in the US

The Fed has responsibility for interest rates in the US, and the responsibility for this rests with the Federal Open Market Committee

(FOMC). Interest rates are controlled through the open-market operations of the Fed. The FOMC decides policy but day-to-day operations are the responsibility of the open-market desk of the New York district Fed.

When the banking system as a whole is short of funds, the Fed supplies liquidity to the market through its open market operations, primarily in repo/reverse repo transactions, or by purchasing Treasury bills or Treasury notes and bonds with a very short time remaining to maturity. Occasionally, the Fed might provide liquidity through discount window lending. The interest rate at which the Fed will deal in the repo market sets the rate for the rest of the market. Its present overnight dealing rate is known as the Fed funds rate. This is the rate referred to when US economic policy is discussed in the press or media.

Guidelines for Money-Market Investing by Corporations

Companies with surplus cash wishing to invest short-term in the money markets can deal either directly or indirectly through a broker or their bank.

Dealing Direct with Market-Making Banks

Large companies with substantial cash surpluses have the ability to speak directly to the main dealing centers of banks, either:

- to make a deposit at a negotiable interest yield, or
- to purchase selected money-market instruments, bills, CDs, CP, repos
- to purchase synthetic or structured securities, such as asset swaps.

The company's treasury department must first ascertain the amount of surplus cash for investment, and the investment period. Guidelines should be drawn for avoiding excessive investment risk. Within the total amount planned, there should be a maximum investment in any single transaction, the size of which should depend on:

- the minimum economic transaction size, given bank charges for money transfers
- the minimum investment size a dealing bank would be willing to accept. The keenest rates will be available only on large investments of at least a few million dollars
- the perceived credit risk in various types of investment. It is

inadvisable, for example, to place too much on deposit with any bank that does not have a high credit rating.

The duration of an investment depends on the amount and timing of the company's cash needs, the volatility and unpredictability of the company's cash flows and the management's judgment about the likely future changes in interest rates, if any, over the planned investment period. The amount and timing of cash needs should be reviewed regularly in a rolling cash forecast. When cash flows are unpredictable, or subject to large outflows or inflows, it could be more appropriate to invest in short-term or marketable instruments that can be converted into cash at short notice should the need arise.

Example
A company has prepared a forecast of its sterling cash flows as follows:

Date	**Cash in £000**	**Cash out £000**	**Cash balance £000**
Week 1			
Start of week			50
Day 1	1,000	100	950
Day 2	850	300	1,500
Day 3	600	500	1,600
Day 4	1,200	1,600	1,200
Day 5	1,500	600	2,100
Week 2	6,000	4,000	4,100
Week 3	5,000	5,000	4,100
Week 4	5,000	5,100	4,000

The finance director has decided to invest the company's temporary cash surpluses in the money markets.

Analysis
The company's cash forecast will extend beyond Week 4, and if the finance director is reasonably confident that the minimum surplus for at least three months from Day 2 of Week 1 will be £1,200,000, he or she

might decide to invest this amount in a money-market instrument such as three-month CDs.

The balance of surplus funds in Week 1 might be held on deposit with a bank at the most favorable rate obtainable for money at call.

From Day 5 of Week 1, the finance director can review the cash situation again, in more detail for Week 2 and beyond, with a view to making further investment decisions for the cash surplus currently expected to build up.

Interest Yield

A company's finance director or treasurer must decide on a target interest-rate yield for investments. This will depend largely on the anticipated level of market interest rates, but also on the skills of the company's dealers in extracting a premium rate from its counterparty banks. One element of skill or judgment is to predict the likely movement in interest rates. The market's expectations of future movements in interest rates, however, are already factored into current money-market rates.

Making an investment at the best time, even during the course of a single day, can earn a company substantial profits. For example, suppose that a company plans to invest £10 million for three months (91 days) in the interbank market and expects to be offered a yield at current LIBID when the transaction is agreed. LIBID at the start of the day might be 5.25% for example. Suppose that LIBID increases during the day to 5.375%, an increase of 12.5 basis points. If the investment is made after the interest-rate rise, the company's interest earnings on the three-month deposit would be higher by £3,116 (£10 million × 0.125% × 91/365).

Beyond the very short term, money-market investment decisions are about choosing the term of investment. These decisions depend on the current and future shape of the yield curve. Speculation on future interest-rate movements is all about judging whether current long-term rates in the market provide an accurate guide to future movements in short-term rates.

The Dealing Process

The company will decide which counterparty banks should be invited to quote. This decision will be determined by a number of factors, such as:

- credit limits (if any) that are applied by the company to the amount of investment with each bank
- market knowledge of which banks are seeking funding of a particular duration that matches the company's short-term investment plans. These banks are likely to offer a higher interest yield than others without the funding need.
- experience and dealing relationships with each bank for various money-market instruments. Companies are likely to use banks whose dealers they know and that have provided good service in the past.

The mechanics of dealing consist of contacting potential counterparty banks and enquiring if they have an interest in, for example, a £10-million deposit for one month and what rate they would pay. The bank will respond in one of four ways.

- It has no interest in the transaction, in which case the conversation ends.
- It is prepared to pay a sub-market price for the funds. This indicates no particular interest in borrowing but a willingness to borrow funds cheaply and reinvest them at a profit.
- It is prepared to pay the market rate (LIBID) for the funds. The corporate dealer then has to judge the chances of finding another bank that would be prepared to pay a premium price. If he/she has already made a number of unsuccessful approaches then acceptance of the market rate would be advised.
- It is prepared to pay a premium over the market rate. The corporate dealer should agreed the transaction at once.

Example

A company telephones four banks and asks whether they have an interest in a £6-million deposit for two months (61 days). The current rate for LIBID is 5.5%.

Alpha Bank offers a rate of 5%. Beta Bank replies that it has no interest at present in such a deposit, but asks the company to try the bank again at a future date when the situation might be different. Gamma Bank offers a rate of 5.6%. Delta Bank, the fourth bank contacted, offers 5.5%.

Gamma Bank has offered the best yield, 0.10% or 10 basis points above LIBID. The interest value of this 10 basis point premium rate is £1,002.74 for the two-month deposit (£6 million × 61/365 × 0.10%).

The company's dealer should have accepted Gamma's offer, without telephoning Delta Bank, unless its target interest yield was even higher than 10 basis points over LIBID. Having telephoned Delta Bank, the company could go back to Gamma Bank and ask again: Gamma's dealer, sensing that the company cannot find a better interest rate elsewhere could now lower its offer by a few basis points.

Investment decisions have to be taken instantly, and so it is advisable to accept an offer immediately from any bank that meets or exceeds the target.

Documentation

Investors normally will be required to confirm a transaction in writing to the bank or financial institution with which it has dealt. Documentation is largely standardized, and is similar for depos (bank deposits) and the purchase of money-market instruments. A typical commercial paper confirmation is illustrated opposite. In this example, the issuing company (Manganese International) is sending a written confirmation to Theta, its dealing bank. The dealing bank also will confirm the issue to Manganese International in an exchange of written confirmations.

If it is a direct deal, the investor sends the confirmation to the bank. If

MANGANESE INTERNATIONAL
COMPANY HEADQUARTERS

MANGANESE INTERNATIONAL
PUBLIC LIMITED COMPANY
COMPANY HEADQUARTERS
P.O. BOX XX
MI HOUSE
BIRMINGHAM
B1 2CD

Telephone: (0999) 666 6666
Facsimile: (0999) 666 6767
Telex: 999999 MAITV

Theta Bank
Threadneedle Street
London

Our Deal no: MCP1234
Date: 27 April 2002

Dear Sirs,

We confirm our issue of Sterling Commercial Paper as follows:

Issue Date:	24 Apr 2002	Yield:	8.492818%
Maturity Date:	20 May 2002	Discount Rate:	8.441752%
Nominal Value:			1,500,000.00
Proceeds:			1,490,980.05

Please remit funds in accordance with standing instructions.

Yours faithfully

Authorized signatory

Authorized signatory

the deal is through a money-market broker or commercial-paper dealer, confirmation goes to the broker. The details of the trade set out in the confirmation should be cross-checked as soon as possible against the confirmation received from the counterparty, (the bank or broker) and certainly before payment is made. This is practical for most investments but not for depos that usually are for same-day value, in which case the cross-check should take place as soon as possible after settlement.

Custody of Investments

Purchased instruments in paper form might require safe custody. This is very important for bearer securities for which physical possession is taken as evidence of ownership. Safe custody is also required for CDs although these may be stored at the company's commercial bank, and for commercial paper but usually this will be warehoused, free of charge, with the bank selling the CP.

Safe custody is not a requirement for those investments for which there is an official register or book-entry system of ownership. As money-market instruments increasingly are issued in dematerialized form, the need for safe custody for money-market instruments will disappear.

Securities purchased under a *repurchase agreement* (repo) also require safe custody unless they are book-entry securities/dematerialized securities. It is fairly common for safe custody to be provided by the counterparty bank to the transaction at no cost. In these cases, however, it is important to insist that the bank arranges physical segregation of the relevant securities because the investor would want to obtain physical possession of them immediately if the bank were to collapse before maturity and settlement of the repo.

Dealing Through Brokers

The money-market broker plays a valuable role in the investment process, whether for a medium-sized company investing all its funds through brokers or for a large company using brokers to complement its direct-dealing activity. The major brokers operating in London have access to a pool of banks far greater than a small company's dealing operation could achieve, and they cover virtually the entire community of active banks. A treasurer or finance director of a large company therefore can check the price efficiency of its direct dealings by routing some of its funds via brokers. Even after deducting a broker's commission, the investment yield on surplus cash may be enhanced, because the broker is more likely than the company to find the marginal borrower willing to pay premium prices.

The corporate dealer has to go through the same process when dealing with a broker as when dealing direct, although it is the broker's task to find a suitable counterparty bank. However, the company can inform the broker if there are any banks with which it does not wish to transact business.

The daily dialogue between client and broker will cover the market position that day including a discussion of changes in interest-rate levels across the yield curve, i.e. for different terms to maturity, and also economic announcements and their possible impact on interest rates. The company's dealer then indicates to the broker the amount available for investment through that broker, the preferred duration of investment and the target interest rate. The broker posts this information in its dealing room for the attention of its interbank dealers. These liaise on a similar basis with banks in the market for borrowing that day.

If the target rate can be wholly or partly achieved by a matching of the interest rate and duration requirements of the corporate client and bank client, the brokers will call each one, i.e. company and bank, and show them the name. This allows each party to give credit clearance to the name of their proposed counterparty by verifying that the counterparty meets their credit criteria and is not already up to its credit limit. If this is satisfactory, and credit clearance usually takes seconds, the transaction is completed.

A company has a duty to play fair by the brokers. To do this it should update the broker if its requirements change during the morning.

- The dealer should set the same interest-rate targets for the same maturity period for each broker with which the company deals. It is unfair to set a higher target interest rate for one broker than for another, for investments with the same maturity.
- The dealer should inform the broker when the company's book is square and no further dealing activity is required.
- A transaction should be refused only on credit grounds or if the corporate dealer has squared the book in the past few seconds and has not yet notified the broker. If the same single transaction is being offered to banks direct as well as through one or more brokers then it should be made clear to the brokers that acceptance of a bid will be dependent on clearance by the company's own in-house dealer, rather than merely subject to a credit check.

Money brokers, properly used, add value by identifying the highest-paying borrowers, and are also a useful conduit for placing large amounts of surplus cash at several banks quickly and price-efficiently. For this reason direct lines to money-broking firms are found even in the dealing rooms of large companies that are used to dealing direct with banks.

Investments by Smaller Companies

Money brokers also are important for small or medium-sized companies because they are prepared to place smaller sums than could be fed into the money markets directly through banks. Amounts as small as £100,000 or even less can be invested at market rates.

Many small companies, however, deal with the liaison officer or dealing room of their normal relationship bank and invest through the bank. Alternatively, they might ask another bank if it is interested in an investment transaction and at what yield.

Some foreign banks with a London office are not active in the London interbank market, and consequently have to borrow funds at a rate in excess of LIBOR in spite of their high credit rating. These banks might try to arrange small transactions with non-bank companies, offering them a better rate than they could obtain on deposits through their relationship bank. They will use a UK correspondent bank to handle the transfer of funds from and to the lending customer. An example of a bank's confirmation of such a transaction is shown overleaf.

Example

The finance director of Foxtrot plc wishes to invest about £5 million in a certificate of deposit for about seven months, and has a contact at a finance house, AC Finance Ltd. The finance house suggests that Foxtrot might wish to buy a secondhand CD, details of which are as follows:

Secondary market
Transaction date: 30 September Year 1

Certificate of Deposit

Issuer	North Bank
Principal amount	£5 million
Term	April 25 Year 1 to April 25 Year 2
Interest rate	5.375%
Purchase price	£5,093,748.37
Term to maturity	209 days
Yield to investor	6.0%

Foxtrot will be required to pay the purchase price for the CD to the finance house that will act as dealer in the transaction. If the CD is in paper form, the finance house will offer to hold the certificate, when it has been purchased, in safekeeping for Foxtrot.

Dealing Guidelines: Large Companies

For large companies with a direct-dealing capability, several guidelines might be useful.

Holland Bank

(Incorporated in the Netherlands with limited liability)
999 MOORGATE, LONDON EC2

TELEPHONE 020 7777 7777

ECHO
HOLDINGS
PLC
ECHO HOUSE
CAVE ROAD
LONDON
W12 1XX

DATE: 3/05/02
REF: 999999/STDEFII/D7777

DEPOSIT

CONFIRM THE SETTLEMENT INSTRUCTIONS FOR YOUR DEPOSIT WITH US:

START	MATURITY	AMOUNT	INTEREST RATE	INT AMOUNT
3/05/02	28/06/02	ST 1,000,000.00	11.625%	17,835.62

TOTAL AMOUNT DUE AT MATURITY: ST 1,017,835.62

AT MATURITY WE HAVE INSTRUCTED:
BETA BANK PUBLIC LIMITED COMPANY
INTERNATIONAL DIVISION
LONDON

WHO WILL MAKE PAYMENT TO:
PLEASE SUPPLY YOUR SETTLEMENT
INSTRUCTIONS

INTEREST PAYMENT DETAILS:
INTEREST WILL BE PAID WITH
THE PRINCIPAL

FOR ACCOUNT OF
YOURSELVES

THIS CONFIRMATION
REQUIRES NO SIGNATURE

Before phoning banks or home-loan companies to ask for an interest rate, a corporate treasurer should calculate the financial impact of each 1/8th% or 1/16th% on the planned transaction. For example, an additional 1/16th% on a £10-million investment for one year equates to £6,250. This is a significant amount, even for large companies. An additional 1/16th% on a £1-million overnight deposit produces only £1.71 of extra interest, and it is not worth spending time trying to extract such a small sum from a bank by insisting on a higher yield.

When a transaction is agreed by phone, the treasurer should have a calculator ready in order to agree the amount of interest receivable or payable. The interest figure verifies three elements in the transaction:

- the amount invested
- the interest rate
- the term of the loan.

A company planning an investment should be comfortable with the additional risks associated with the higher yields on offer from any investment that might seem attractive. There is no such thing as a free lunch in money markets and yields on different investments reflect the market's collective perception of the amount that various lenders should expect to pay for borrowed funds. One notable example in the London market was the collapse of the Bank of Credit and Commerce International (BCCI) in 1991. Depositors who lost money should have been aware that the large premium return on BCCI deposits reflected the money-market's perception of the bank's higher investment risk.

Equally important is to spread the investment risk over a number of different banks or instruments.

Money-market dealing should be avoided if possible after 2 p.m., because liquidity falls rapidly as market participants square their position and stop dealing. Any late receipts after 2 p.m. are best dealt out immediately, into an overnight deposit with the bank into which the receipt has cleared, to avoid an external bank transfer late in the day. The money then can be invested in a longer-term instrument, if required, the next morning when market liquidity is better.

Summary

Dealing practise and relationships vary according to the size of company and the type of investments it wants to make. Except for relatively small sums, companies should consider alternative methods of investing in the money markets in addition to dealing through their normal relationship bank. By using a variety of investment options and dealing contracts, a company can expect to improve its income without incurring unnecessary credit risks.

Glossary

Acceptance
Acceptance by the drawee on a term bill of exchange, recognizing the obligation to pay the stated sum on the specified date.

Bank bill
A bill of exchange drawn on a bank and accepted by that bank.

Banker's acceptances (BAs)
A financing arrangement whereby a bank provides short-term finance to a company by accepting bills of exchange drawn on it, discounts the bills (sells them in the market) and gives the proceeds to the company. The financing arrangement provides for the company to draw bills on the bank up to a specified limit for outstanding bills. When each bill matures, the bank makes the payment, but requires the company to make the funds available for reimbursement.

Basis point
One hundredth of 1% (0.01%); therefore 100 basis points = 1%.

Bearer security
A security for which there is no official register of ownership. Where bearer securities are issued in paper form, possession of the certificate or bill is taken as proof of ownership. Bearer securities therefore are more easily negotiable (salable) than registered securities, for which ownership and transfer of ownership is recorded in an official register. Bearer securities can be held in computerized book-entry form, and a computer record will be the proof of ownership.

Bid rate
The quoted interest rate at which a bank is willing to buy/accept deposits.

Bill of exchange
An unconditional order in writing from one person or company to another, requiring the addressee, the drawee, to pay a specified sum of money on demand (a sight bill) or at a future date (a term bill).

Book entry
Computer record of the ownership of securities or financial instruments. Book entry systems are maintained by central securities depositories, such as the DTCC, Clearstream, Euroclear and Crest.

Broker
A person who acts as an agent or go-between, bringing together principals who wish to deal, e.g. borrow and lend, in the money markets at mutually agreed prices, but who does not act as a principal to any transaction.

Central securities depository (CSD)
An organization that is responsible for holding computerized records of the ownership of securities and/or financial instruments. Transfers of the securities or instruments are settled through the CSD. Each participant, e.g. investor, has one or more securities/investments accounts, and a cash memorandum account. Payments for purchases of securities/instruments are arranged through the system. Each participant must use a participant settlement bank that has a link to the system. CSDs include the international CSDs, Clearstream and Euroclear, and national CSDs such as Crest in the UK.

Certificate of deposit (CD)
A documentation issued by a bank certificating that an amount of money has been deposited and that the holder of the documentation will be entitled to the money with interest on a stated date.

Central Moneymarkets Office (CMO)
An office established by the Bank of England in 1989 to provide new settlement facilities for sterling money-market transactions in bearer securities. Sold to Crestco, the owner of the Crest system, in 1999. Settlement of wholesale transactions in money-market instruments was transferred to the Crest system in 2001.

Commercial paper (CP)
Unsecured loan notes, issued by an agent on behalf of an issuing company, promising to pay the bearer a stated amount at maturity. CP has a maturity of one day to 270 days in the US or seven days to 364 days in the UK. CP may be issued in either dematerialized or paper form. Companies issue CP within the framework of a CP program, up to a specified limit for CP outstanding at any given time.

Counterparty
The other party to a contract.

Crest
Central securities depository in the UK. Ownership of shares and bonds are recorded in book-entry form within Crest, with participants having securities accounts. Transfers of securities are settled through the Crest system. From 2001, ownership of money-market instruments will be recorded in Crest, and wholesale transactions in these instruments will be settled through Crest by DVP.

Currency swap
An agreement between two parties, possibly lasting up to ten years or even longer, to exchange a series of payments in one currency for a series of payments in a second currency, usually at regular intervals over the term of the swap. These are payments of interest at an agreed rate on a nominal principal amount of one currency, in exchange for payments of interest at another rate on a second currency. Also there will be an exchange of the principal currency amounts at the end of the term of the swap.

Debt Management Office
Office of the government (the Treasury) responsible for issuing bills, notes and bonds on behalf of the UK government, having taken over this responsibility from the Bank of England in 1999.

Derivatives
Financial instruments derived from an underlying cash-market loan, investment or purchase transaction. They include interest-rate options, futures, swaps and FRAs.

Depo
Bank deposit.

Discount basis
Basis for trading money-market instruments such as bills of exchange, that will be redeemed at par value at maturity. Discount instruments are issued and traded at a price below their face value (at a discount). An interest rate is reflected in the size of discount and term to maturity.

Discount house
A bank operating in the London markets and a member of the London Discount Markets Association. At one time, discount houses played a key role in the money markets.

DVP
Delivery versus payment. An arrangement for settling a transaction in securities or money-market instruments whereby the seller must deliver the instruments to the buyer, and simultaneously the buyer must pay for them.

Eurocommercial paper (ECP)
Commercial paper issued in eurocurrencies, particularly the dollar.

Eurocurrency
Funds deposited and lent in a currency outside the country of the currency's origin.

Euromarket
The market for borrowing and lending/depositing eurocurrencies.

Fed funds
Funds held by US banks and depository institutions with their district Federal Reserve Bank. There is a large interbank market for borrowing and lending surplus Fed funds – the Fed-funds market.

Fed-funds rate
A repo rate for overnight transactions, applied by the Fed in its open-market operations, in order to control interest rates in the US money markets.

Federal Open Market Committee (FOMC)
Committee of the Fed responsible for influencing the state of the US economy, through control over short-term interest rates.

Federal Reserve Bank
Central bank of the US, with a governing board in Washington and 12 district Federal Reserve Banks.

Fedwire
Same-day, funds-transfer service for Fed funds.

Fixed-rate interest
Interest paid at the same rate for the full term of a loan or investment. Money-market loans, being short term, generally are at fixed-rate interest.

Floating-rate interest
Interest paid at a variable rate over the term of a loan or investment. The rate is reset at periodic rollover dates, normally in line with current market rates of interest.

FRN
Floating-Rate Note. A medium-term security paying interest on a variable-rate basis, normally subject to a minimum floor level. The interest rate payable is reset periodically.

Hedge
Take action to reduce or eliminate an exposure.

Instrument
A general term used in the financial markets to describe methods of borrowing or investing. The term is widely used in particular to describe money-market securities.

ISMA
International Securities Market Association. Self-regulating body of international banks, based in Europe, that formulates regulations and documentation for the international securities markets, including the repo markets.

LIBID
London Interbank Bid Rate. Theoretically the rate in the interbank money market at which top-rated (prime) banks will deposit funds with another prime bank. LIBID normally is 1/8 of 1% below LIBOR.

LIBOR
London Interbank Offered Rate. Theoretically the rate in the interbank money market at which top-rated (prime) banks will lend to another prime bank with a high credit rating.

LIMEAN
The average of the LIBOR and LIBID rates for a given maturity, e.g. one month, three months etc.

Liquid market
A term used to describe a market in which investors can buy and resell securities or other instruments on demand and at fair, competitive prices.

Market maker
A dealer or trader who makes a market by consistently quoting selling and buying prices (bid and offered rates), and is willing to trade at those prices.

Medium-term note (MTN)
A loan note issued by a company, with a maturity of between one and five years.

Offer rate
The rate at which a dealer is willing to sell or a bank is willing to lend.

Placement
A eurocurrency deposit placed by one bank with another bank.

Primary market
The market in which new issues of financial instruments/securities are sold initially.

Repo
See Sale-and-repurchase agreement.

Reverse repo
A sale-and-repurchase agreement in which a dealer buys securities from a customer and at the same time promises to sell them back at a date in the near future, at an agreed price.

Sale-and-repurchase agreement (repo)
The sale of securities for current delivery and a simultaneous agreement to repurchase them at a future date, at a higher price. A repo in effect is a secured short-term loan with the security provided by high-quality money-market or capital-market instruments.

Secondary market
A market for buying and selling securities in the period between their issue and maturity. A liquid secondary market enhances the attractiveness of financial instruments/securities to investors.

Security
A negotiable instrument giving evidence of a debt or equity obligation by its issue to the owner of the security.

Short-term
In most financial markets, a term of less than one year.

Sight bill
See Bill of Exchange.

Spread
The difference between a market-maker's borrowing and lending rates or buying and selling prices.

Subordinated debt
Debt securities that rank behind other debts in the event of a liquidation of the issuing company. Claims of subordinated debt holders on the assets of the issuing company will be satisfied only if the claims of creditors ranking ahead of them are first satisfied in full. Subordinated debt carries a greater credit risk for the investor and so will offer a higher yield.

Tap
A method of issuing securities as and when required, often in irregular amounts. The name refers to the turning on and off of a tap, i.e. releasing securities to the market and then cutting off the supply, and releasing more later.

Term bill
See Bill of Exchange.

Trade bill (commercial bill)
Bill drawn by one non-bank company on another company, typically demanding payment for a trade debt.

Treasury bill
Short-term IOU issued by a government to finance short-term cash deficiencies. A Treasury bill promises to pay a certain amount at maturity to the holder. In the US, Treasury bills are issued with maturities of 91 days, 182 days or 364 days.

USCP

Commercial paper issued in dollars in the US money markets.

Yield

Rate of return on an investment, expressed as an interest rate per annum.

Index